Wine Making Journal

Table Of Contents

D1613754

Abbreviations

Alc. Tol.	Alcohol Tolerance
C	Celsius
F	Fahrenheit
Lbs	Pounds
SO2	Sulfur Dioxide
Spc. Grv.	Specific Gravity
TA	Tartaric Acid
Tbsp	Tablespoon
tsp	Teaspoon

Author: Adam T. Courtney
ISBN: 978-1-4303-0329-9
Cover Photo By: Michael Giguere
                 www.michaelgiguerephotography.com
Feedback: winejournal@yahoo.com
Websites: www.WineMakingJournal.com
                 myspace.com/winejournal
                 Facebook.com Group : Wine Making Journal
Copyright: 2006 by Adam T. Courtney

Special Thanks To: Rob Simonar, Michael Giguere, Rikki Pahlow, Derrick Casper, John Herbes, Julie Wessley, Matt Orlowski, Jack Keller, House of Homebrew, my wife Christina, and of course everyone who has tasted my wine (the good and the bad). This journal was made with no thanks to Justin Buehler.

Celsius To Fahrenheit

$$F = (C * 1.8) + 32$$

C	F	C	F	C	F	C	F	C	F	C	F	C	F
-20	-4.0	0	32.0	20	68.0	40	104.0	60	140.0	80	176.0	100	212.0
-19	-2.2	1	33.8	21	69.8	41	105.8	61	141.8	81	177.8	101	213.8
-18	-0.4	2	35.6	22	71.6	42	107.6	62	143.6	82	179.6	102	215.6
-17	1.4	3	37.4	23	73.4	43	109.4	63	145.4	83	181.4	103	217.4
-16	3.2	4	39.2	24	75.2	44	111.2	64	147.2	84	183.2	104	219.2
-15	5.0	5	41.0	25	77.0	45	113.0	65	149.0	85	185.0	105	221.0
-14	6.8	6	42.8	26	78.8	46	114.8	66	150.8	86	186.8	106	222.8
-13	8.6	7	44.6	27	80.6	47	116.6	67	152.6	87	188.6	107	224.6
-12	10.4	8	46.4	28	82.4	48	118.4	68	154.4	88	190.4	108	226.4
-11	12.2	9	48.2	29	84.2	49	120.2	69	156.2	89	192.2	109	228.2
-10	14.0	10	50.0	30	86.0	50	122.0	70	158.0	90	194.0	110	230.0
-9	15.8	11	51.8	31	87.8	51	123.8	71	159.8	91	195.8	111	231.8
-8	17.6	12	53.6	32	89.6	52	125.6	72	161.6	92	197.6	112	233.6
-7	19.4	13	55.4	33	91.4	53	127.4	73	163.4	93	199.4	113	235.4
-6	21.2	14	57.2	34	93.2	54	129.2	74	165.2	94	201.2	114	237.2
-5	23.0	15	59.0	35	95.0	55	131.0	75	167.0	95	203.0	115	239.0
-4	24.8	16	60.8	36	96.8	56	132.8	76	168.8	96	204.8	116	240.8
-3	26.6	17	62.6	37	98.6	57	134.6	77	170.6	97	206.6	117	242.6
-2	28.4	18	64.4	38	100.4	58	136.4	78	172.4	98	208.4	118	244.4
-1	30.2	19	66.2	39	102.2	59	138.2	79	174.2	99	210.2	119	246.2
												120	248.0

Fahrenheit To Celsius

$$C = (F - 32) / 1.8$$

F	C	F	C	F	C	F	C	F	C	F	C	F	C
0	-17.8	32	0.0	64	17.8	96	35.6	128	53.3	160	71.1	192	88.9
1	-17.2	33	0.6	65	18.3	97	36.1	129	53.9	161	71.7	193	89.4
2	-16.7	34	1.1	66	18.9	98	36.7	130	54.4	162	72.2	194	90.0
3	-16.1	35	1.7	67	19.4	99	37.2	131	55.0	163	72.8	195	90.6
4	-15.6	36	2.2	68	20.0	100	37.8	132	55.6	164	73.3	196	91.1
5	-15.0	37	2.8	69	20.6	101	38.3	133	56.1	165	73.9	197	91.7
6	-14.4	38	3.3	70	21.1	102	38.9	134	56.7	166	74.4	198	92.2
7	-13.9	39	3.9	71	21.7	103	39.4	135	57.2	167	75.0	199	92.8
8	-13.3	40	4.4	72	22.2	104	40.0	136	57.8	168	75.6	200	93.3
9	-12.8	41	5.0	73	22.8	105	40.6	137	58.3	169	76.1	201	93.9
10	-12.2	42	5.6	74	23.3	106	41.1	138	58.9	170	76.7	202	94.4
11	-11.7	43	6.1	75	23.9	107	41.7	139	59.4	171	77.2	203	95.0
12	-11.1	44	6.7	76	24.4	108	42.2	140	60.0	172	77.8	204	95.6
13	-10.6	45	7.2	77	25.0	109	42.8	141	60.6	173	78.3	205	96.1
14	-10.0	46	7.8	78	25.6	110	43.3	142	61.1	174	78.9	206	96.7
15	-9.4	47	8.3	79	26.1	111	43.9	143	61.7	175	79.4	207	97.2
16	-8.9	48	8.9	80	26.7	112	44.4	144	62.2	176	80.0	208	97.8
17	-8.3	49	9.4	81	27.2	113	45.0	145	62.8	177	80.6	209	98.3
18	-7.8	50	10.0	82	27.8	114	45.6	146	63.3	178	71.1	210	98.9
19	-7.2	51	10.6	83	28.3	115	46.1	147	63.9	179	81.7	212	99.4
20	-6.7	52	11.1	84	28.9	116	46.7	148	64.4	180	82.2	213	100.0
21	-6.1	53	11.7	85	29.4	117	47.2	149	65.0	181	82.8	214	100.6
22	-5.6	54	12.2	86	30.0	118	47.8	150	65.6	182	83.3	215	101.1
23	-5.0	55	12.8	87	30.6	119	48.3	151	66.1	183	83.9	216	101.7
24	-4.4	56	13.3	88	31.1	120	48.9	152	66.7	184	84.4	217	102.2
25	-3.9	57	13.9	89	31.7	121	49.4	153	67.2	185	85.0	218	102.8
26	-3.3	58	14.4	90	32.2	122	50.0	154	67.8	186	85.6	219	103.3
27	-2.8	59	15.0	91	32.8	123	40.6	155	68.3	187	86.1	220	103.9
28	-2.2	60	15.6	92	33.3	124	51.1	156	68.9	188	86.7	221	104.4
29	-1.7	61	16.1	93	33.9	125	51.7	157	69.4	189	87.2	222	105.0
30	-1.1	62	16.7	94	34.4	126	52.2	158	70.0	190	87.8	223	106.1
31	-0.6	63	17.2	95	35.0	127	52.8	159	70.6	191	88.3	224	106.7

Measurement Conversions

1 tablespoon = 3 teaspoons
1 cup = 16 tablespoons = 48 teaspoons = 8 ounces
1 pint = 2 cups = 16 fluid ounces = 1 pound
1 quart = 4 cups = 2 pints = 32 fluid ounces = 2 pounds

tsp	Tbsp	Cup	Pint	Ounce	Pound	Quart	tsp	Tbsp	Cup	Pint	Ounce	Pound	Quart
1							49						
2							50						
3	1						51	17					
4							52						
5							53						
6	2	1/8		1			54	18	1 1/8		9		
7							55						
8							56						
9	3						57	19					
10							58						
11							59						
12	4	1/4	1/8	2	1/8	1/16	60	20	1 1/4	5/8	10	5/8	5/16
13							61						
14							62						
15	5						63	21					
16		1/3					64		1 1/3	2/3			
17							65						
18	6	3/8		3			66	22	1 3/8		11		
19							67						
20							68						
21	7						69	23					
22							70						
23							71						
24	8	1/2	1/4	4	1/4	1/8	72	24	1 1/2	3/4	12	3/4	3/8
25							73						
26							74						
27	9						75	25					
28							76						
29							77						
30	10	5/8		5			78	26	1 5/8		13		
31							79						
32		2/3	1/3				80		1 2/3				
33	11						81	27					
34							82						
35							83						
36	12	3/4		6	3/8	3/16	84	28	1 3/4		14	7/8	7/16
37							85						
38							86						
39	13						87	29					
40							88						
41							89						
42	14	7/8		7			90	30	1 7/8		15		
43							91						
44							92						
45	15						93	31					
46							94						
47							95						
48	16	1	1/2	8	1/2	1/4	96	32	2	1	16	1	1/2

Hydrometer Conversion

Specific Gravity	Bailing Brix	Potential Alcohol	Sugar Ounces Per Gallon
1.000	0	0.0%	0
1.004	1	0.6%	1.4
1.008	2	1.1%	2.8
1.012	3	1.7%	4.3
1.016	4	2.2%	5.7
1.019	5	2.6%	6.8
1.023	6	3.2%	8.2
1.027	7	3.7%	9.6
1.031	8	4.3%	11.0
1.035	9	4.8%	12.4
1.039	10	5.4%	13.9
1.043	11	5.9%	15.3
1.047	12	6.5%	16.7
1.050	13	6.9%	17.8
1.054	14	7.4%	19.2
1.058	15	8.0%	20.6
1.062	16	8.6%	22.0
1.066	17	9.1%	23.5
1.070	18	9.7%	24.9
1.074	19	10.2%	26.3
1.078	20	10.8%	27.7
1.081	21	11.2%	28.8
1.085	22	11.7%	30.2
1.089	23	12.3%	31.6
1.093	24	12.8%	33.1

Hydrometer Temperature Correction

F	C	Adjustment
32	0	Subtract 1.6
41	5	Subtract 1.3
50	10	Subtract 0.8
60	15.6	Correct
68	20	Add 1.0
77	25	Add 2.2
86	30	Add 3.5
95	35	Add 5.0
104	40	Add 6.8
113	45	Add 8.8
122	50	Add 11.0
131	55	Add 13.3
140	60	Add 15.9

Wine Additives - Teaspoons Per Ounce

Ascorbic Acid	6 Teaspoons
Acid Blend	6 Teaspoons
Calcium Carbonate	12 Teaspoons
Citric Acid	6 Teaspoons
Gelatin	8 Teaspoons
Malic Acid	6 Teaspoons
Polyclar	27 Teaspoons
Stabilizer	8 Teaspoons
Sugar	6 Teaspoons
Tannin	12 Teaspoons
Tartaric Acid	6 Teaspoons
Yeast Energizer	9 Teaspoons
Yeast Nutrient	5 Teaspoons

Bung Sizes

Bung Size	Bottom Diameter (cm)	Top Diameter (cm)
2	1.6	1.9
3	1.8	2.2
5.5	2.4	2.8
6	2.7	3.2
6.5	2.8	3.4
7	3	3.8
7.5	3.1	3.9
8	3.3	4.1
8.5	3.6	4.3
9.5	3.8	4.6
10	4.3	5
10.5	4.5	5.3
11	4.9	5.6
11.5	5	6.3

Yeast Quick Reference

Brand	Yeast	Temp (F)	Alc. Tol.	Flocculation	Notes
Lalvin	ICV D-47	50-86	14%	Medium	_____
Lalvin	Bourgovin RC 212	59-86	14%	Low	_____
Lalvin	71-B	59-86	14%	Medium	_____
Lalvin	KIV-1116	59-86	16%	Low	_____
Lalvin	EC-1118	45-95	18%	Low	_____
Red Star	Pasteur Red	64-86	16%	Low	_____
Red Star	Montrachet	59-86	13%	Low	_____
Red Star	Cote des Blancs	64-86	12-14%	Low	_____
Red Star	Pasteur Champagne	59-86	13-15%	Low-Medium	_____
Red Star	Premier Cuvee	45-95	18%	Low	_____
Red Star	Flor Sherry	59-86	18-20%	Low	_____
White Labs	Champagne	70-75	17%	Low	_____
White Labs	Sweet Mead and Wine	70-75	15%	Low	_____
White Labs	English Cider	68-75	14%	Medium	_____
White Labs	Chardonnay White Wine	50-90	14%	Low	_____
White Labs	Merlot Red Wine Yeast	60-90	18%	Low	_____
White Labs	Cabernet Red Wine Yeast	60-90	16%	Low	_____
Wyeast	Pasteur Champagne	55-75	17%	Low-Medium	_____
Wyeast	Dry Mead	55-75	18%	Low-Medium	_____
Wyeast	Sweet Mead	60-75	11%	Low-Medium	_____
Wyeast	Sake #9	60-75	16%	Low-Medium	_____
Wyeast	Chablis	55-75	12-13%	High	_____
Wyeast	Rudisheimer	55-75	12-13%	Medium	_____
Wyeast	Assmannhausen	60-90	12-14%	Medium-High	_____
Wyeast	Pasteur Red	55-90	14%	Medium-High	_____
Wyeast	Bordeaux	55-90	14%	Low-Medium	_____
Wyeast	Eau de Vie	65-80	21%	Low	_____
Wyeast	Cider	60-75	12%	High	_____
Wyeast	Portwine	60-90	14%	Low-Medium	_____
Wyeast	Steinberg	55-75	12-13%	Medium-High	_____

_____

_____

_____

_____

_____

Your Favorite Recipes

Ingredients: 1-1/4 lbs granulated sugar

2 cans Welch's 100% frozen grape concentrate

2 tsp acid blend

1 tsp pectic enzyme

1 tsp yeast nutrient

water to make 1 gallon

Name: Welch's Frozen Grape Juice Wine

Yeast: Red Star Premier Curvee

or Lalvin EC-1118 wine yeast

Directions: Bring 1 quart water to boil and dissolve the sugar in the water. Remove from heat and add frozen concentrate. Add additional water to make one gallon and pour into secondary. Add remaining ingredients except yeast. Cover with napkin fastened with rubber band and set aside 12 hours. Add activated wine yeast and recover with napkin. When active fermentation slows down (about 5 days), fit airlock. When clear, rack, top up and refit airlock. After additional 30 days, stabilize, sweeten if desired and rack into bottles.

Notes: [Jack Keller's adaptation of a friend's recipe]

Extra Special Thanks To:

Jack Keller's "The Winemaking Home Page" at http://winemaking.jackkeller.net/

Jack's website has been a useful resource for all of my home winemaking needs.

Ingredients:

Name:

Yeast:

Directions:

Notes:

Your Favorite Recipes

Ingredients: _____

_____

_____

_____

_____

Name: _____

Yeast: _____

_____

_____

_____

_____

Directions: _____

_____

_____

_____

_____

_____

_____

Notes: _____

_____

_____

_____

_____

_____

Ingredients: _____

_____

_____

_____

_____

_____

Name: _____

Yeast: _____

_____

_____

_____

_____

Directions: _____

_____

_____

_____

_____

_____

_____

Notes: _____

_____

_____

_____

_____

_____

Your Favorite Recipes

Ingredients: 10/15/08

Seyval Blanc from
2008 made from skins
added sugar had 5gal.

Not bad taste now, actually

Directions:
Distilled 3 quarts had 3 gal left over
in carboy.

Notes:

Name: Grappa

Yeast:

Ingredients:

Directions:

Notes:

Name:

Yeast:

Ingredients: 10/15/08

Name:

Yeast:

Directions: Distilled 2 gal of Chamberine leaving 3 gal to bottle. 2½ quarts +

Notes:

Ingredients:

Name:

Yeast:

Directions:

Notes:

Your Favorite Recipes

Ingredients: _____   **Name:** _____
_____   **Yeast:** _____
_____   _____
_____   _____
_____   _____
_____   _____

Directions: _____
_____
_____
_____
_____
_____

Notes: _____
_____
_____
_____
_____

Ingredients: _____   **Name:** _____
_____   **Yeast:** _____
_____   _____
_____   _____
_____   _____
_____   _____

Directions: _____
_____
_____
_____
_____
_____

Notes: _____
_____
_____
_____
_____

Your Favorite Recipes

Ingredients:
_____

_____

_____

_____

_____

Name:
_____

Yeast:
_____

_____

_____

_____

Directions:
_____

_____

_____

_____

_____

Notes:
_____

_____

_____

_____

_____

Ingredients:
_____

_____

_____

_____

_____

Name:
_____

Yeast:
_____

_____

_____

_____

Directions:
_____

_____

_____

_____

_____

Notes:
_____

_____

_____

_____

_____

Your Favorite Recipes

Ingredients: _____   Name: _____

_____   Yeast: _____

_____   _____

_____   _____

_____   _____

_____   _____

Directions: _____

_____

_____

_____

_____

_____

Notes: _____

_____

_____

_____

_____

Ingredients: _____   Name: _____

_____   Yeast: _____

_____   _____

_____   _____

_____   _____

_____   _____

Directions: _____

_____

_____

_____

_____

Notes: _____

_____

_____

_____

_____

Your Favorite Recipes

Ingredients: _____

_____

_____

_____

_____

Name: _____

Yeast: _____

_____

_____

_____

_____

Directions: _____

_____

_____

_____

_____

_____

_____

Notes: _____

_____

_____

_____

_____

_____

Ingredients: _____

_____

_____

_____

_____

Name: _____

Yeast: _____

_____

_____

_____

_____

Directions: _____

_____

_____

_____

_____

_____

Notes: _____

_____

_____

_____

_____

Your Favorite Recipes

Ingredients: _____

_____

_____

_____

_____

_____

Name: _____

Yeast: _____

_____

_____

_____

_____

Directions: _____

_____

_____

_____

_____

_____

Notes: _____

_____

_____

_____

_____

Ingredients: _____

_____

_____

_____

_____

_____

Name: _____

Yeast: _____

_____

_____

_____

_____

Directions: _____

_____

_____

_____

_____

_____

Notes: _____

_____

_____

_____

_____

Ingredients:

Name:

Yeast:

Directions:

Notes:

Ingredients:

Name:

Yeast:

Directions:

Notes:

Primary Fermentation 9/12/08   #: 1

Ingredients:

Name: Seyval Blanc

Spc. Grv. Before Correcton: 17¾

Sugar Added: 1.5#s

Spc. Grv. After Correction: 21.9

pH Before Correction:

pH Correction:

pH After Correction:

TA Before:

TA Correction:

Yeast: 1 package Blanc de Blanc

TA After:

Gallons Of Must: 4¾

Total SO2:

Notes: 9/8/08 lots of rot in bunches; Brix at 19.8 average.
9/11/08 picked all Seyval – total 82 lbs
9/12/08 Crushed & added ¾ of ¼ tsp Pectic Enzyme
Brix of total = 17¾° - 18°
9/13/08 added 3 tsps yeast nutrient, yeast, ready to go
. Lots of sediment as squeezed. Must had to get
juice – actually re squeezed.

Secondary Fermentation

Date:	Racked:	Spc. Grv.:	pH:	SO2:	Gallons:	Additions:
9/28/08	☑	.998			4	none

Notes: Froze 8oz of fermented juice to fill up later
at subsequent rackings

| 1/1/21 | ☐ | | | | | |

Notes: rack again

| __/__/__ | ☐ | | | | | |

Notes:

| __/__/__ | ☐ | | | | | |

Notes:

| __/__/__ | ☐ | | | | | |

Notes:

| __/__/__ | ☐ | | | | | |

Notes:

Bottling ____/____/____

Spc. Grv. Before Sweeting: _____

Sugar Added: _____

Final pH: _____

Final SO2: _____

Final TA: _____

Of Bottles: _____

% Alcohol By Volume: _____

Notes: _____

_____

_____

_____

_____

_____

_____

Attach
Label
Here

Tasting

Color: _____

Body / Flavor: _____

Finish: _____

Tasting Notes: _____

_____

_____

_____

_____

_____

_____

Other Notes: _____

_____

_____

_____

_____

_____

_____

_____

_____

Primary Fermentation ___/___/___   #: _____   Name: _Izaminute_

Ingredients: _____

_____

_____

_____

_____

_____

_____

Yeast: _____

Gallons Of Must: _____

Spc. Grv. Before Correcton: _____

Sugar Added: _____

Spc. Grv. After Correction: _____

pH Before Correction: _____

pH Correction: _____

pH After Correction: _____

TA Before: _____

TA Correction: _____

TA After: _____

Total SO2: _____

Notes: 9/8/08 Beautiful bunches - almost no rt. Brix 18°
9/23/08 All bunches GONE. Stripped bare.
Why? Opossum, squirrels, racoon?
Vines netted, scare balloons, plus 7 or 8 yellow
jacket traps. Maybe shouldn't have waited
from 9/8 to 9/23??

Secondary Fermentation 10/13 Caught opossum in box trap who bought
grapes as bait in vineyard. Released
at a distance.

Date:	Racked:	Spc. Grv.:	pH:	SO2:	Gallons:	Additions:
___/___/___	☐					
Notes:						
___/___/___	☐					
Notes:						
___/___/___	☐					
Notes:						
___/___/___	☐					
Notes:						
___/___/___	☐					
Notes:						
___/___/___	☐					
Notes:						

Bottling _____ / _____ / _____

Spc. Grv. Before Sweeting: _____

Sugar Added: _____

Final pH: _____

Final SO2: _____

Final TA: _____

Of Bottles: _____

% Alcohol By Volume: _____

Notes: _____

_____

_____

_____

_____

_____

Attach
Label
Here

Tasting

Color: _____

Body / Flavor: _____

Finish: _____

Tasting Notes: _____

_____

_____

_____

_____

_____

_____

Other Notes: _____

_____

_____

_____

_____

_____

_____

_____

Primary Fermentation 9/17/08   #: 1   Name: Apple Wine

Ingredients: bought 5 1 gallon bottle
for Melick's of fresh pressed
apple juice

Spc. Grv. Before Correcton:

Sugar Added: never?

Spc. Grv. After Correction: 1.089   178

pH Before Correction:

pH Correction:

pH After Correction:

TA Before:

TA Correction:

Yeast: Blanc de Blanc

TA After:

Gallons Of Must: 5 gal

Total SO2:

Notes: recipe from p. 201 "Home Wine maker's comp."
froze a quart to add later

Secondary Fermentation

Date:	Racked:	Spc. Grv.:	pH:	SO2:	Gallons:	Additions:
10/7/08	☑	.996			5	¼ teaspoon P

Notes: added fresh juice, was frozen, to top up -
maybe 8 oz balance frozen

/ /	☐					

Notes:

12/2/08	☐					

Notes: Rack wine for last time

12/2/08	☑	1.002			5	12 oz water

Notes: Was clear but after racking became cloudy again.
Very good taste but needs aging.

/ /	☐					

Notes:

/ /	☐					

Notes:

Bottling _____/_____/_____

Spc. Grv. Before Sweeting: _____

Sugar Added: _____

Final pH: _____

Final SO2: _____

Final TA: _____

Of Bottles: _____

% Alcohol By Volume: _____

Attach
Label
Here

Notes: _____

_____

_____

_____

_____

_____

_____

Tasting

Color: _____

Body / Flavor: _____

Finish: _____

Tasting Notes: _____

_____

_____

_____

_____

_____

_____

Other Notes: _____

_____

_____

_____

_____

_____

_____

_____

_____

_____

Primary Fermentation 10/22/08   #: _____

Name: Pinot Gris

Ingredients:

5 gal container sent
from Walkers on the shores
of Lake Erie.

Spc. Grv. Before Correcton: 21°

Sugar Added: None

Spc. Grv. After Correction: ——

pH Before Correction:

pH Correction:

pH After Correction:

TA Before:

TA Correction:

Yeast: Blanc de Blanc

TA After:

Gallons Of Must: 5

Total SO2: 50 ppm

Notes: Added 1¼ teaspoons of yeast nutrient
Put most in 5 gal jug then put remainder
in gal jug.

Juice was very sweet to taste almost
syrupy.

Secondary Fermentation

Date:	Racked:	Spc. Grv.:	pH:	SO2:	Gallons:	Additions:
11/8/08	☑	1.022			1	frozen cider

Notes: Transferred set aside frozen juice + parted
gallon to fill up 5 gal jug added 2/3 cup water
still active fermentation - Harsh taste.

	☐					

Notes:

Date:	Racked:	Spc. Grv.:	pH:	SO2:	Gallons:	Additions:
12/17/08	☑	1.24				also: 14 oz of water, 1 bottle P.G from Home

Notes: Taste syrupy + slightly bitter. Will bitter
be sweet + fear. Still fermenting so slowly put in
syrup

	☐					

Notes:

___/___/___	☐					

Notes:

___/___/___	☐					

Notes:

Bottling _____/_____/_____

Spc. Grv. Before Sweeting: _____

Sugar Added: _____

Final pH: _____

Final SO2: _____

Final TA: _____

Of Bottles: _____

% Alcohol By Volume: _____

Notes: _____

_____

_____

_____

_____

_____

_____

Attach
Label
Here

Tasting

Color: _____

Body / Flavor: _____

Finish: _____

Tasting Notes: _____

_____

_____

_____

_____

_____

_____

Other Notes: _____

_____

_____

_____

_____

_____

_____

_____

_____

Primary Fermentation 10 / 7 / 09   # ~~Seyval Blanc~~   Name: Seyval Blanc

Ingredients:

Grape bunches (big but
full of rot & dead grapes.
Need to prune back growth
and cluster thin big time,
Over cropped - no time to
sort 18 lbs grapes chucked
out.

Yeast: Blanc de Blanc

Gallons Of Must: 7 gal

Spc. Grv. Before Correcton:	1.5,5°
Sugar Added:	4.1 lbs
Spc. Grv. After Correction:	1.84
pH Before Correction:	
pH Correction:	
pH After Correction:	
TA Before:	
TA Correction:	
TA After:	
Total SO2:	

Notes: Pressed each cake hard. Added 4 tsp of
yeast nutrient & 1/2 package yeast. Very
gray green color to must.
After crushing added Pectin + SO2 then let sit
over night covered by cloth. Then pressed.

Secondary Fermentation

Date:	Racked:	Spc. Grv.:	pH:	SO2:	Gallons:	Additions:
10 / 21 / 09	☑	.9996			5	plus 2 coke

Notes: Lots of sediment - Wine had acid taste bottles 3/4 full
& I fear may be spoiled. Very dry! Taste as above

Date:	Racked:	Spc. Grv.:	pH:	SO2:	Gallons:	Additions:
___ / ___ / ___	☐					

Notes:

| ___ / ___ / ___ | ☐ | | | | | |

Notes:

| ___ / ___ / ___ | ☐ | | | | | |

Notes:

| ___ / ___ / ___ | ☐ | | | | | |

Notes:

| ___ / ___ / ___ | ☐ | | | | | |

Notes:

Bottling _____/_____/_____

Spc. Grv. Before Sweeting: _____

Sugar Added: _____

Final pH: _____

Final SO2: _____

Final TA: _____

Of Bottles: _____

% Alcohol By Volume: _____

Notes: _____

_____

_____

_____

_____

_____

_____

Attach
Label
Here

Tasting

Color: _____

Body / Flavor: _____

Finish: _____

Tasting Notes: _____

_____

_____

_____

_____

_____

_____

Other Notes: _____

_____

_____

_____

_____

_____

_____

_____

Primary Fermentation 10, 9, 09   #: _____

Ingredients:

Egal of Melick's Cider -
fresh pres. Very sweet +
delicious

_____

_____

_____

_____

Yeast: Red Star Premier Cuvée

Gallons Of Must: _____

Notes: Use recipe, fresh p. 201 Home Wine etc. (did added
grape tannin as had n't last year.

_____

_____

_____

Name: Apple Wine

Spc. Grv. Before Correcton: 1.052

Sugar Added: almost 6 lbs.

Spc. Grv. After Correction: 1.086

pH Before Correction: _____

pH Correction: _____

pH After Correction: _____

TA Before: _____

TA Correction: _____

TA After: _____

Total SO2: _____

Secondary Fermentation

Date:	Racked:	Spc. Grv.:	pH:	SO2:	Gallons:	Additions:
___/___/___	☐	_____	_____	_____	_____	_____
Notes:						
___/___/___	☐	_____	_____	_____	_____	_____
Notes:						
___/___/___	☐	_____	_____	_____	_____	_____
Notes:						
___/___/___	☐	_____	_____	_____	_____	_____
Notes:						
___/___/___	☐	_____	_____	_____	_____	_____
Notes:						
___/___/___	☐	_____	_____	_____	_____	_____
Notes:						

Bottling _____ / _____ / _____

Spc. Grv. Before Sweeting: _____

Sugar Added: _____

Final pH: _____

Final SO2: _____

Final TA: _____

Of Bottles: _____

% Alcohol By Volume: _____

Notes: _____

_____

_____

_____

_____

Attach
Label
Here

_____

_____

Tasting

Color: _____

Body / Flavor: _____

Finish: _____

Tasting Notes: _____

_____

_____

_____

_____

_____

_____

Other Notes: _____

_____

_____

_____

_____

_____

_____

_____

_____

Primary Fermentation 10, 7, 09   #: _____

Ingredients: Hardly any grapes
Next boy - big changes.

Pick squeezed, and
bottled.

_____

Yeast: Cote de Blanc

Gallons Of Must: 3⅓ gal

Notes: Pick out all rotten ones - not much any
black rot.

Name: Trammmunette

Spc. Grv. Before Correcton: 16.5 or 1067

Sugar Added: small amount

Spc. Grv. After Correction: 1.085

pH Before Correction: _____

pH Correction: _____

pH After Correction: _____

TA Before: _____

TA Correction: _____

TA After: _____

Total SO2: _____

Secondary Fermentation

Date:	Racked:	Spc. Grv.:	pH:	SO2:	Gallons:	Additions:
10,22,09	☐	.998		1=1.5L 1=750m		More

Notes: taster pleasant bitter p
Notes: _____

____/____/____ ☐ ____ ____ ____ ____ ____
Notes: _____

____/____/____ ☐ ____ ____ ____ ____ ____
Notes: _____

____/____/____ ☐ ____ ____ ____ ____ ____
Notes: _____

____/____/____ ☐ ____ ____ ____ ____ ____
Notes: _____

____/____/____ ☐ ____ ____ ____ ____ ____
Notes: _____

Bottling _____/_____/_____

Spc. Grv. Before Sweeting: _____

Sugar Added: _____

Final pH: _____

Final SO2: _____

Final TA: _____

Of Bottles: _____

% Alcohol By Volume: _____

Attach
Label
Here

Notes: _____

_____

_____

_____

_____

_____

_____

Tasting

Color: _____

Body / Flavor: _____

Finish: _____

Tasting Notes: _____

_____

_____

_____

_____

_____

_____

Other Notes: _____

_____

_____

_____

_____

_____

_____

_____

_____

Primary Fermentation _____/_____/_____ #: _____ Name: _____

Ingredients: _____ Spc. Grv. Before Correcton: _____

_____ Sugar Added: _____

_____ Spc. Grv. After Correction: _____

_____ pH Before Correction: _____

_____ pH Correction: _____

_____ pH After Correction: _____

_____ TA Before: _____

_____ TA Correction: _____

Yeast: _____ TA After: _____

Gallons Of Must: _____ Total SO2: _____

Notes: _____

_____

_____

_____

_____

_____

Secondary Fermentation

Date:	Racked:	Spc. Grv.:	pH:	SO2:	Gallons:	Additions:
____/____/____	☐	_____	_____	_____	_____	_____
Notes:						
____/____/____	☐	_____	_____	_____	_____	_____
Notes:						
____/____/____	☐	_____	_____	_____	_____	_____
Notes:						
____/____/____	☐	_____	_____	_____	_____	_____
Notes:						
____/____/____	☐	_____	_____	_____	_____	_____
Notes:						
____/____/____	☐	_____	_____	_____	_____	_____
Notes:						

Bottling _____/_____/_____

Spc. Grv. Before Sweeting: _____

Sugar Added: _____

Final pH: _____

Final SO2: _____

Final TA: _____

Of Bottles: _____

% Alcohol By Volume: _____

Attach
Label
Here

Notes: _____

_____

_____

_____

_____

_____

_____

Tasting

Color: _____

Body / Flavor: _____

Finish: _____

Tasting Notes: _____

_____

_____

_____

_____

_____

_____

Other Notes: _____

_____

_____

_____

_____

_____

_____

_____

Primary Fermentation _____/_____/_____   #: _____

Ingredients: _____

_____

_____

_____

_____

_____

_____

Yeast: _____

Gallons Of Must: _____

Notes: _____

_____

_____

_____

_____

_____

Name: _____

Spc. Grv. Before Correcton: _____

Sugar Added: _____

Spc. Grv. After Correction: _____

pH Before Correction: _____

pH Correction: _____

pH After Correction: _____

TA Before: _____

TA Correction: _____

TA After: _____

Total SO2: _____

Secondary Fermentation

Date:	Racked:	Spc. Grv.:	pH:	SO2:	Gallons:	Additions:
_____/_____/_____	☐	_____	_____	_____	_____	_____

Notes: _____

| _____/_____/_____ | ☐ | _____ | _____ | _____ | _____ | _____ |

Notes: _____

| _____/_____/_____ | ☐ | _____ | _____ | _____ | _____ | _____ |

Notes: _____

| _____/_____/_____ | ☐ | _____ | _____ | _____ | _____ | _____ |

Notes: _____

| _____/_____/_____ | ☐ | _____ | _____ | _____ | _____ | _____ |

Notes: _____

| _____/_____/_____ | ☐ | _____ | _____ | _____ | _____ | _____ |

Notes: _____

Bottling _____/_____/_____

Spc. Grv. Before Sweeting: _____

Sugar Added: _____

Final pH: _____

Final SO2: _____

Final TA: _____

Of Bottles: _____

% Alcohol By Volume: _____

Notes: _____
_____
_____
_____
_____

_____
_____

Attach
Label
Here

Tasting

Color: _____

Body / Flavor: _____

Finish: _____

Tasting Notes: _____

_____
_____
_____
_____
_____
_____

Other Notes: _____

_____
_____
_____
_____
_____
_____
_____

Primary Fermentation _____/_____/_____   #: _____   Name: _____

Ingredients: _____   Spc. Grv. Before Correcton: _____

_____   Sugar Added: _____

_____   Spc. Grv. After Correction: _____

_____   pH Before Correction: _____

_____   pH Correction: _____

_____   pH After Correction: _____

_____   TA Before: _____

_____   TA Correction: _____

Yeast: _____   TA After: _____

Gallons Of Must: _____   Total SO2: _____

Notes: _____

_____

_____

_____

_____

_____

Secondary Fermentation

Date:	Racked:	Spc. Grv.:	pH:	SO2:	Gallons:	Additions:
____/____/____	☐	_____	_____	_____	_____	_____

Notes: _____

| ____/____/____ | ☐ | _____ | _____ | _____ | _____ | _____ |

Notes: _____

| ____/____/____ | ☐ | _____ | _____ | _____ | _____ | _____ |

Notes: _____

| ____/____/____ | ☐ | _____ | _____ | _____ | _____ | _____ |

Notes: _____

| ____/____/____ | ☐ | _____ | _____ | _____ | _____ | _____ |

Notes: _____

| ____/____/____ | ☐ | _____ | _____ | _____ | _____ | _____ |

Notes: _____

Bottling _____/_____/_____

Spc. Grv. Before Sweeting: _____

Sugar Added: _____

Final pH: _____

Final SO2: _____

Final TA: _____

Of Bottles: _____

% Alcohol By Volume: _____

Attach
Label
Here

Notes: _____

_____

_____

_____

_____

_____

_____

Tasting

Color: _____

Body / Flavor: _____

Finish: _____

Tasting Notes: _____

_____

_____

_____

_____

_____

_____

Other Notes: _____

_____

_____

_____

_____

_____

_____

_____

Primary Fermentation _____/_____/_____   #: _____   Name: _____

Ingredients: _____   Spc. Grv. Before Correcton: _____

_____   Sugar Added: _____

_____   Spc. Grv. After Correction: _____

_____   pH Before Correction: _____

_____   pH Correction: _____

_____   pH After Correction: _____

_____   TA Before: _____

_____   TA Correction: _____

Yeast: _____   TA After: _____

Gallons Of Must: _____   Total SO2: _____

Notes: _____

_____

_____

_____

_____

_____

_____

Secondary Fermentation

Date:	Racked:	Spc. Grv.:	pH:	SO2:	Gallons:	Additions:
_____/_____/_____	☐	_____	_____	_____	_____	_____
Notes:						
_____/_____/_____	☐	_____	_____	_____	_____	_____
Notes:						
_____/_____/_____	☐	_____	_____	_____	_____	_____
Notes:						
_____/_____/_____	☐	_____	_____	_____	_____	_____
Notes:						
_____/_____/_____	☐	_____	_____	_____	_____	_____
Notes:						
_____/_____/_____	☐	_____	_____	_____	_____	_____
Notes:						

Bottling ____/____/____

Spc. Grv. Before Sweeting: _____

Sugar Added: _____

Final pH: _____

Final SO2: _____

Final TA: _____

Of Bottles: _____

% Alcohol By Volume: _____

Notes: _____

_____

_____

_____

_____

_____

_____

Attach
Label
Here

Tasting

Color: _____

Body / Flavor: _____

Finish: _____

Tasting Notes: _____

_____

_____

_____

_____

_____

_____

Other Notes: _____

_____

_____

_____

_____

_____

_____

_____

Primary Fermentation _____/_____/_____   #: _____

Ingredients: _____

_____

_____

_____

_____

_____

_____

Yeast: _____

Gallons Of Must: _____

Notes: _____

_____

_____

_____

_____

_____

Name: _____

Spc. Grv. Before Correcton: _____

Sugar Added: _____

Spc. Grv. After Correction: _____

pH Before Correction: _____

pH Correction: _____

pH After Correction: _____

TA Before: _____

TA Correction: _____

TA After: _____

Total SO2: _____

Secondary Fermentation

Date:	Racked:	Spc. Grv.:	pH:	SO2:	Gallons:	Additions:
_____/_____/_____	☐	_____	_____	_____	_____	_____
Notes:						
_____/_____/_____	☐	_____	_____	_____	_____	_____
Notes:						
_____/_____/_____	☐	_____	_____	_____	_____	_____
Notes:						
_____/_____/_____	☐	_____	_____	_____	_____	_____
Notes:						
_____/_____/_____	☐	_____	_____	_____	_____	_____
Notes:						
_____/_____/_____	☐	_____	_____	_____	_____	_____
Notes:						

Bottling _____ / _____ / _____

Spc. Grv. Before Sweeting: _____

Sugar Added: _____

Final pH: _____

Final SO2: _____

Final TA: _____

Of Bottles: _____

% Alcohol By Volume: _____

Notes: _____

_____

_____

_____

_____

_____

_____

Attach
Label
Here

Tasting

Color: _____

Body / Flavor: _____

Finish: _____

Tasting Notes: _____

_____

_____

_____

_____

_____

_____

_____

Other Notes: _____

_____

_____

_____

_____

_____

_____

_____

_____

Primary Fermentation _____/_____/_____   #: _____   Name: _____

Ingredients: _____   Spc. Grv. Before Correcton: _____

_____   Sugar Added: _____

_____   Spc. Grv. After Correction: _____

_____   pH Before Correction: _____

_____   pH Correction: _____

_____   pH After Correction: _____

_____   TA Before: _____

_____   TA Correction: _____

Yeast: _____   TA After: _____

Gallons Of Must: _____   Total SO2: _____

Notes: _____

_____

_____

_____

_____

_____

Secondary Fermentation

Date:	Racked:	Spc. Grv.:	pH:	SO2:	Gallons:	Additions:
____/____/____	☐	_____	_____	_____	_____	_____
Notes:						
____/____/____	☐	_____	_____	_____	_____	_____
Notes:						
____/____/____	☐	_____	_____	_____	_____	_____
Notes:						
____/____/____	☐	_____	_____	_____	_____	_____
Notes:						
____/____/____	☐	_____	_____	_____	_____	_____
Notes:						
____/____/____	☐	_____	_____	_____	_____	_____
Notes:						

Bottling __ __ / ____ / ____

Spc. Grv. Before Sweeting: _____

Sugar Added: _____

Final pH: _____

Final SO2: _____

Final TA: _____

Of Bottles: _____

% Alcohol By Volume: _____

Notes: _____

_____

_____

_____

_____

_____

_____

Attach
Label
Here

Tasting

Color: _____

Body / Flavor: _____

Finish: _____

Tasting Notes: _____

_____

_____

_____

_____

_____

_____

Other Notes: _____

_____

_____

_____

_____

_____

_____

_____

_____

Primary Fermentation ____/____/____   #: _____   Name: _____

Ingredients: _____   Spc. Grv. Before Correcton: _____

_____   Sugar Added: _____

_____   Spc. Grv. After Correction: _____

_____   pH Before Correction: _____

_____   pH Correction: _____

_____   pH After Correction: _____

_____   TA Before: _____

_____   TA Correction: _____

Yeast: _____   TA After: _____

Gallons Of Must: _____   Total SO2: _____

Notes: _____

_____

_____

_____

_____

_____

Secondary Fermentation

Date:	Racked:	Spc. Grv.:	pH:	SO2:	Gallons:	Additions:
___/___/___	☐	_____	_____	_____	_____	_____

Notes: _____

| ___/___/___ | ☐ | _____ | _____ | _____ | _____ | _____ |

Notes: _____

| ___/___/___ | ☐ | _____ | _____ | _____ | _____ | _____ |

Notes: _____

| ___/___/___ | ☐ | _____ | _____ | _____ | _____ | _____ |

Notes: _____

| ___/___/___ | ☐ | _____ | _____ | _____ | _____ | _____ |

Notes: _____

| ___/___/___ | ☐ | _____ | _____ | _____ | _____ | _____ |

Notes: _____

Bottling _____/_____/_____

Spc. Grv. Before Sweeting: _____

Sugar Added: _____

Final pH: _____

Final SO2: _____

Final TA: _____

Of Bottles: _____

% Alcohol By Volume: _____

Notes: _____
_____
_____
_____
_____

_____
_____

Attach
Label
Here

Tasting

Color: _____

Body / Flavor: _____

Finish: _____

Tasting Notes: _____
_____
_____
_____
_____
_____
_____

Other Notes: _____
_____
_____
_____
_____
_____
_____
_____
_____

Primary Fermentation _____/_____/_____   #: _____   Name: _____

Ingredients: _____   Spc. Grv. Before Correcton: _____

_____   Sugar Added: _____

_____   Spc. Grv. After Correction: _____

_____   pH Before Correction: _____

_____   pH Correction: _____

_____   pH After Correction: _____

_____   TA Before: _____

_____   TA Correction: _____

Yeast: _____   TA After: _____

Gallons Of Must: _____   Total SO2: _____

Notes: _____

_____

_____

_____

_____

_____

Secondary Fermentation

Date:	Racked:	Spc. Grv.:	pH:	SO2:	Gallons:	Additions:
_____/_____/_____	☐	_____	_____	_____	_____	_____

Notes: _____

| _____/_____/_____ | ☐ | _____ | _____ | _____ | _____ | _____ |

Notes: _____

| _____/_____/_____ | ☐ | _____ | _____ | _____ | _____ | _____ |

Notes: _____

| _____/_____/_____ | ☐ | _____ | _____ | _____ | _____ | _____ |

Notes: _____

| _____/_____/_____ | ☐ | _____ | _____ | _____ | _____ | _____ |

Notes: _____

| _____/_____/_____ | ☐ | _____ | _____ | _____ | _____ | _____ |

Notes: _____

Bottling ____/____/____

Spc. Grv. Before Sweeting: _____

Sugar Added: _____

Final pH: _____

Final SO2: _____

Final TA: _____

Of Bottles: _____

% Alcohol By Volume: _____

Notes: _____

_____

_____

_____

_____

_____

_____

Attach Label Here

Tasting

Color: _____

Body / Flavor: _____

Finish: _____

Tasting Notes: _____

_____

_____

_____

_____

_____

_____

Other Notes: _____

_____

_____

_____

_____

_____

_____

_____

Primary Fermentation ____/____/____   #: _____   Name: _____

Ingredients: _____   Spc. Grv. Before Correcton: _____

_____   Sugar Added: _____

_____   Spc. Grv. After Correction: _____

_____   pH Before Correction: _____

_____   pH Correction: _____

_____   pH After Correction: _____

_____   TA Before: _____

_____   TA Correction: _____

Yeast: _____   TA After: _____

Gallons Of Must: _____   Total SO2: _____

Notes: _____

_____

_____

_____

_____

_____

Secondary Fermentation

Date:	Racked:	Spc. Grv.:	pH:	SO2:	Gallons:	Additions:
____/____/____	☐	_____	_____	_____	_____	_____

Notes: _____

| ____/____/____ | ☐ | _____ | _____ | _____ | _____ | _____ |

Notes: _____

| ____/____/____ | ☐ | _____ | _____ | _____ | _____ | _____ |

Notes: _____

| ____/____/____ | ☐ | _____ | _____ | _____ | _____ | _____ |

Notes: _____

| ____/____/____ | ☐ | _____ | _____ | _____ | _____ | _____ |

Notes: _____

| ____/____/____ | ☐ | _____ | _____ | _____ | _____ | _____ |

Notes: _____

Bottling _____/_____/_____

Spc. Grv. Before Sweeting: _____

Sugar Added: _____

Final pH: _____

Final SO2: _____

Final TA: _____

Of Bottles: _____

% Alcohol By Volume: _____

Attach
Label
Here

Notes: _____

_____

_____

_____

_____

_____

Tasting

Color: _____

Body / Flavor: _____

Finish: _____

Tasting Notes: _____

_____

_____

_____

_____

_____

_____

Other Notes: _____

_____

_____

_____

_____

_____

_____

_____

Primary Fermentation _____/_____/_____   #: _____   Name: _____

Ingredients: _____   Spc. Grv. Before Correcton: _____

_____   Sugar Added: _____

_____   Spc. Grv. After Correction: _____

_____   pH Before Correction: _____

_____   pH Correction: _____

_____   pH After Correction: _____

_____   TA Before: _____

_____   TA Correction: _____

Yeast: _____   TA After: _____

Gallons Of Must: _____   Total SO2: _____

Notes: _____

_____

_____

_____

_____

_____

Secondary Fermentation

Date:	Racked:	Spc. Grv.:	pH:	SO2:	Gallons:	Additions:
___/___/___	☐	_____	_____	_____	_____	_____

Notes: _____

| ___/___/___ | ☐ | _____ | _____ | _____ | _____ | _____ |

Notes: _____

| ___/___/___ | ☐ | _____ | _____ | _____ | _____ | _____ |

Notes: _____

| ___/___/___ | ☐ | _____ | _____ | _____ | _____ | _____ |

Notes: _____

| ___/___/___ | ☐ | _____ | _____ | _____ | _____ | _____ |

Notes: _____

| ___/___/___ | ☐ | _____ | _____ | _____ | _____ | _____ |

Notes: _____

Bottling _____/_____/_____

Spc. Grv. Before Sweeting: _____

Sugar Added: _____

Final pH: _____

Final SO2: _____

Final TA: _____

Of Bottles: _____

% Alcohol By Volume: _____

Notes: _____

_____

_____

_____

_____

Attach
Label
Here

_____

_____

Tasting

Color: _____

Body / Flavor: _____

Finish: _____

Tasting Notes: _____

_____

_____

_____

_____

_____

Other Notes: _____

_____

_____

_____

_____

_____

_____

_____

Primary Fermentation _____/_____/_____ #: _____   Name: _____

Ingredients: _____   Spc. Grv. Before Correcton: _____
_____   Sugar Added: _____
_____   Spc. Grv. After Correction: _____
_____   pH Before Correction: _____
_____   pH Correction: _____
_____   pH After Correction: _____
_____   TA Before: _____
_____   TA Correction: _____
Yeast: _____   TA After: _____
Gallons Of Must: _____   Total SO2: _____
Notes: _____
_____
_____
_____
_____
_____

Secondary Fermentation

Date:	Racked:	Spc. Grv.:	pH:	SO2:	Gallons:	Additions:
_____/_____/_____	☐	_____	_____	_____	_____	_____
Notes:						
_____/_____/_____	☐	_____	_____	_____	_____	_____
Notes:						
_____/_____/_____	☐	_____	_____	_____	_____	_____
Notes:						
_____/_____/_____	☐	_____	_____	_____	_____	_____
Notes:						
_____/_____/_____	☐	_____	_____	_____	_____	_____
Notes:						
_____/_____/_____	☐	_____	_____	_____	_____	_____
Notes:						

Bottling _____/_____/_____

Spc. Grv. Before Sweeting: _____

Sugar Added: _____

Final pH: _____

Final SO2: _____

Final TA: _____

Of Bottles: _____

% Alcohol By Volume: _____

Attach
Label
Here

Notes: _____

_____

_____

_____

_____

_____

_____

Tasting

Color: _____

Body / Flavor: _____

Finish: _____

Tasting Notes: _____

_____

_____

_____

_____

_____

_____

Other Notes: _____

_____

_____

_____

_____

_____

_____

_____

Primary Fermentation ____/____/____   #: _____

Ingredients:

_____

_____

_____

_____

_____

_____

Yeast:

Gallons Of Must:

Notes:

_____

_____

_____

_____

_____

Name: _____

Spc. Grv. Before Correcton: _____

Sugar Added: _____

Spc. Grv. After Correction: _____

pH Before Correction: _____

pH Correction: _____

pH After Correction: _____

TA Before: _____

TA Correction: _____

TA After: _____

Total SO2: _____

Secondary Fermentation

Date:	Racked:	Spc. Grv.:	pH:	SO2:	Gallons:	Additions:
___/___/___	☐					
Notes:						
___/___/___	☐					
Notes:						
___/___/___	☐					
Notes:						
___/___/___	☐					
Notes:						
___/___/___	☐					
Notes:						
___/___/___	☐					
Notes:						

Bottling   ___/____/____

Spc. Grv. Before Sweeting: _____

Sugar Added: _____

Final pH: _____

Final SO2: _____

Final TA: _____

Of Bottles: _____

% Alcohol By Volume: _____

Notes: _____

_____

_____

_____

_____

_____

_____

Attach
Label
Here

Tasting

Color: _____

Body / Flavor: _____

Finish: _____

Tasting Notes: _____

_____

_____

_____

_____

_____

_____

Other Notes: _____

_____

_____

_____

_____

_____

_____

_____

Primary Fermentation _____/_____/_____   #: _____   Name: _____

Ingredients: _____

_____

_____

_____

_____

_____

_____

_____

Yeast: _____

Gallons Of Must: _____

Notes: _____

_____

_____

_____

_____

_____

_____

Spc. Grv. Before Correcton: _____

Sugar Added: _____

Spc. Grv. After Correction: _____

pH Before Correction: _____

pH Correction: _____

pH After Correction: _____

TA Before: _____

TA Correction: _____

TA After: _____

Total SO2: _____

Secondary Fermentation

Date:	Racked:	Spc. Grv.:	pH:	SO2:	Gallons:	Additions:
_____/_____/_____	☐	_____	_____	_____	_____	_____

Notes: _____

| _____/_____/_____ | ☐ | _____ | _____ | _____ | _____ | _____ |

Notes: _____

| _____/_____/_____ | ☐ | _____ | _____ | _____ | _____ | _____ |

Notes: _____

| _____/_____/_____ | ☐ | _____ | _____ | _____ | _____ | _____ |

Notes: _____

| _____/_____/_____ | ☐ | _____ | _____ | _____ | _____ | _____ |

Notes: _____

| _____/_____/_____ | ☐ | _____ | _____ | _____ | _____ | _____ |

Notes: _____

Bottling _____/_____/_____

Spc. Grv. Before Sweeting: _____

Sugar Added: _____

Final pH: _____

Final SO2: _____

Final TA: _____

Of Bottles: _____

% Alcohol By Volume: _____

Notes: _____

_____

_____

_____

_____

_____

_____

Attach
Label
Here

Tasting

Color: _____

Body / Flavor: _____

Finish: _____

Tasting Notes: _____

_____

_____

_____

_____

_____

Other Notes: _____

_____

_____

_____

_____

_____

_____

_____

Primary Fermentation _____/_____/_____   #: _____

Ingredients: _____

_____

_____

_____

_____

_____

_____

Yeast: _____

Gallons Of Must: _____

Notes: _____

_____

_____

_____

_____

_____

Name: _____

Spc. Grv. Before Correcton: _____

Sugar Added: _____

Spc. Grv. After Correction: _____

pH Before Correction: _____

pH Correction: _____

pH After Correction: _____

TA Before: _____

TA Correction: _____

TA After: _____

Total SO2: _____

Secondary Fermentation

Date:	Racked:	Spc. Grv.:	pH:	SO2:	Gallons:	Additions:
_____/_____/_____	☐	_____	_____	_____	_____	_____

Notes: _____

| _____/_____/_____ | ☐ | _____ | _____ | _____ | _____ | _____ |

Notes: _____

| _____/_____/_____ | ☐ | _____ | _____ | _____ | _____ | _____ |

Notes: _____

| _____/_____/_____ | ☐ | _____ | _____ | _____ | _____ | _____ |

Notes: _____

| _____/_____/_____ | ☐ | _____ | _____ | _____ | _____ | _____ |

Notes: _____

| _____/_____/_____ | ☐ | _____ | _____ | _____ | _____ | _____ |

Notes: _____

Bottling ____/____/____

Spc. Grv. Before Sweeting: _____

Sugar Added: _____

Final pH: _____

Final SO2: _____

Final TA: _____

Of Bottles: _____

% Alcohol By Volume: _____

Notes: _____

_____

_____

_____

_____

Attach
Label
Here

_____

_____

Tasting

Color: _____

Body / Flavor: _____

Finish: _____

Tasting Notes: _____

_____

_____

_____

_____

_____

_____

Other Notes: _____

_____

_____

_____

_____

_____

_____

_____

Primary Fermentation ____/____/____   #: _____   Name: _____

Ingredients: _____   Spc. Grv. Before Correcton: _____

_____   Sugar Added: _____

_____   Spc. Grv. After Correction: _____

_____   pH Before Correction: _____

_____   pH Correction: _____

_____   pH After Correction: _____

_____   TA Before: _____

_____   TA Correction: _____

Yeast: _____   TA After: _____

Gallons Of Must: _____   Total SO2: _____

Notes: _____

_____

_____

_____

_____

_____

_____

Secondary Fermentation

Date:	Racked:	Spc. Grv.:	pH:	SO2:	Gallons:	Additions:
___/___/___	☐	_____	_____	_____	_____	_____
Notes:						
___/___/___	☐	_____	_____	_____	_____	_____
Notes:						
___/___/___	☐	_____	_____	_____	_____	_____
Notes:						
___/___/___	☐	_____	_____	_____	_____	_____
Notes:						
___/___/___	☐	_____	_____	_____	_____	_____
Notes:						
___/___/___	☐	_____	_____	_____	_____	_____
Notes:						

Bottling _____/_____/_____

Spc. Grv. Before Sweeting: _____

Sugar Added: _____

Final pH: _____

Final SO2: _____

Final TA: _____

Of Bottles: _____

% Alcohol By Volume: _____

Notes: _____

_____

_____

_____

_____

_____

Attach
Label
Here

Tasting

Color: _____

Body / Flavor: _____

Finish: _____

Tasting Notes: _____

_____

_____

_____

_____

_____

_____

Other Notes: _____

_____

_____

_____

_____

_____

_____

_____

Primary Fermentation ____/____/____   #: _____   Name: _____

Ingredients: _____   Spc. Grv. Before Correcton: _____

_____   Sugar Added: _____

_____   Spc. Grv. After Correction: _____

_____   pH Before Correction: _____

_____   pH Correction: _____

_____   pH After Correction: _____

_____   TA Before: _____

_____   TA Correction: _____

Yeast: _____   TA After: _____

Gallons Of Must: _____   Total SO2: _____

Notes: _____

_____

_____

_____

_____

_____

_____

Secondary Fermentation

Date:	Racked:	Spc. Grv.:	pH:	SO2:	Gallons:	Additions:
___/___/___	☐	_____	_____	_____	_____	_____

Notes: _____

| ___/___/___ | ☐ | _____ | _____ | _____ | _____ | _____ |

Notes: _____

| ___/___/___ | ☐ | _____ | _____ | _____ | _____ | _____ |

Notes: _____

| ___/___/___ | ☐ | _____ | _____ | _____ | _____ | _____ |

Notes: _____

| ___/___/___ | ☐ | _____ | _____ | _____ | _____ | _____ |

Notes: _____

| ___/___/___ | ☐ | _____ | _____ | _____ | _____ | _____ |

Notes: _____

Bottling ___/___/___

Spc. Grv. Before Sweeting: _____

Sugar Added: _____

Final pH: _____

Final SO2: _____

Final TA: _____

Of Bottles: _____

% Alcohol By Volume: _____

Notes: _____

_____

_____

_____

_____

_____

_____

Attach
Label
Here

Tasting

Color: _____

Body / Flavor: _____

Finish: _____

Tasting Notes: _____

_____

_____

_____

_____

_____

_____

Other Notes: _____

_____

_____

_____

_____

_____

_____

_____

Primary Fermentation _____/_____/_____   #: _____

Ingredients: _____

_____

_____

_____

_____

_____

_____

Yeast: _____

Gallons Of Must: _____

Notes: _____

_____

_____

_____

_____

_____

_____

Name: _____

Spc. Grv. Before Correcton: _____

Sugar Added: _____

Spc. Grv. After Correction: _____

pH Before Correction: _____

pH Correction: _____

pH After Correction: _____

TA Before: _____

TA Correction: _____

TA After: _____

Total SO2: _____

Secondary Fermentation

Date:	Racked:	Spc. Grv.:	pH:	SO2:	Gallons:	Additions:
____/____/____	☐	_____	_____	_____	_____	_____
Notes:						
____/____/____	☐	_____	_____	_____	_____	_____
Notes:						
____/____/____	☐	_____	_____	_____	_____	_____
Notes:						
____/____/____	☐	_____	_____	_____	_____	_____
Notes:						
____/____/____	☐	_____	_____	_____	_____	_____
Notes:						
____/____/____	☐	_____	_____	_____	_____	_____
Notes:						

Bottling _____/_____/_____

Spc. Grv. Before Sweeting: _____

Sugar Added: _____

Final pH: _____

Final SO2: _____

Final TA: _____

Of Bottles: _____

% Alcohol By Volume: _____

Attach
Labe
Here

Notes: _____

_____

_____

_____

_____

_____

_____

Tasting

Color: _____

Body / Flavor: _____

Finish: _____

Tasting Notes: _____

_____

_____

_____

_____

_____

_____

Other Notes: _____

_____

_____

_____

_____

_____

_____

_____

Primary Fermentation ____/____/____   #: _____   Name: _____

Ingredients: _____   Spc. Grv. Before Correcton: _____

_____   Sugar Added: _____

_____   Spc. Grv. After Correction: _____

_____   pH Before Correction: _____

_____   pH Correction: _____

_____   pH After Correction: _____

_____   TA Before: _____

_____   TA Correction: _____

Yeast: _____   TA After: _____

Gallons Of Must: _____   Total SO2: _____

Notes: _____

_____

_____

_____

_____

_____

_____

Secondary Fermentation

Date:	Racked:	Spc. Grv.:	pH:	SO2:	Gallons:	Additions:
____/____/____	☐	_____	_____	_____	_____	_____
Notes:						
____/____/____	☐	_____	_____	_____	_____	_____
Notes:						
____/____/____	☐	_____	_____	_____	_____	_____
Notes:						
____/____/____	☐	_____	_____	_____	_____	_____
Notes:						
____/____/____	☐	_____	_____	_____	_____	_____
Notes:						
____/____/____	☐	_____	_____	_____	_____	_____
Notes:						

Bottling _____ / _____ / _____

Spc. Grv. Before Sweeting: _____

Sugar Added: _____

Final pH: _____

Final SO2: _____

Final TA: _____

Of Bottles: _____

% Alcohol By Volume: _____

Attach
Label
Here

Notes: _____

_____

_____

_____

_____

_____

Tasting

Color: _____

Body / Flavor: _____

Finish: _____

Tasting Notes: _____

_____

_____

_____

_____

_____

_____

Other Notes: _____

_____

_____

_____

_____

_____

_____

Primary Fermentation _____/_____/_____   #: _____   Name: _____

Ingredients: _____   Spc. Grv. Before Correcton: _____

_____   Sugar Added: _____

_____   Spc. Grv. After Correction: _____

_____   pH Before Correction: _____

_____   pH Correction: _____

_____   pH After Correction: _____

_____   TA Before: _____

_____   TA Correction: _____

Yeast: _____   TA After: _____

Gallons Of Must: _____   Total SO2: _____

Notes: _____

_____

_____

_____

_____

_____

Secondary Fermentation

Date:	Racked:	Spc. Grv.:	pH:	SO2:	Gallons:	Additions:
____/____/____	☐	_____	_____	_____	_____	_____
Notes:						
____/____/____	☐	_____	_____	_____	_____	_____
Notes:						
____/____/____	☐	_____	_____	_____	_____	_____
Notes:						
____/____/____	☐	_____	_____	_____	_____	_____
Notes:						
____/____/____	☐	_____	_____	_____	_____	_____
Notes:						
____/____/____	☐	_____	_____	_____	_____	_____
Notes:						

Bottling _____ / _____ / _____

Spc. Grv. Before Sweeting: _____

Sugar Added: _____

Final pH: _____

Final SO2: _____

Final TA: _____

Of Bottles: _____

% Alcohol By Volume: _____

Attach
Label
Here

Notes: _____

_____

_____

_____

_____

_____

_____

Tasting

Color: _____

Body / Flavor: _____

Finish: _____

Tasting Notes: _____

_____

_____

_____

_____

_____

_____

Other Notes: _____

_____

_____

_____

_____

_____

_____

Primary Fermentation _____/_____/_____   #: _____   Name: _____

Ingredients: _____   Spc. Grv. Before Correcton: _____

_____   Sugar Added: _____

_____   Spc. Grv. After Correction: _____

_____   pH Before Correction: _____

_____   pH Correction: _____

_____   pH After Correction: _____

_____   TA Before: _____

_____   TA Correction: _____

Yeast: _____   TA After: _____

Gallons Of Must: _____   Total SO2: _____

Notes: _____

_____

_____

_____

_____

_____

Secondary Fermentation

Date:	Racked:	Spc. Grv.:	pH:	SO2:	Gallons:	Additions:
____/____/____	☐	_____	_____	_____	_____	_____

Notes: _____

| ____/____/____ | ☐ | _____ | _____ | _____ | _____ | _____ |

Notes: _____

| ____/____/____ | ☐ | _____ | _____ | _____ | _____ | _____ |

Notes: _____

| ____/____/____ | ☐ | _____ | _____ | _____ | _____ | _____ |

Notes: _____

| ____/____/____ | ☐ | _____ | _____ | _____ | _____ | _____ |

Notes: _____

| ____/____/____ | ☐ | _____ | _____ | _____ | _____ | _____ |

Notes: _____

Bottling _____/_____/_____

Spc. Grv. Before Sweeting: _____

Sugar Added: _____

Final pH: _____

Final SO2: _____

Final TA: _____

Of Bottles: _____

% Alcohol By Volume: _____

Attach
Label
Here

Notes: _____

_____

_____

_____

_____

_____

_____

Tasting

Color: _____

Body / Flavor: _____

Finish: _____

Tasting Notes: _____

_____

_____

_____

_____

_____

_____

Other Notes: _____

_____

_____

_____

_____

_____

_____

_____

Primary Fermentation _____/_____/_____   #: _____

Ingredients: _____

_____

_____

_____

_____

_____

_____

Yeast: _____

Gallons Of Must: _____

Notes: _____

_____

_____

_____

_____

_____

_____

Name: _____

Spc. Grv. Before Correcton: _____

Sugar Added: _____

Spc. Grv. After Correction: _____

pH Before Correction: _____

pH Correction: _____

pH After Correction: _____

TA Before: _____

TA Correction: _____

TA After: _____

Total SO2: _____

Secondary Fermentation

Date:	Racked:	Spc. Grv.:	pH:	SO2:	Gallons:	Additions:
_____/_____/_____	☐	_____	_____	_____	_____	_____
Notes:						
_____/_____/_____	☐	_____	_____	_____	_____	_____
Notes:						
_____/_____/_____	☐	_____	_____	_____	_____	_____
Notes:						
_____/_____/_____	☐	_____	_____	_____	_____	_____
Notes:						
_____/_____/_____	☐	_____	_____	_____	_____	_____
Notes:						
_____/_____/_____	☐	_____	_____	_____	_____	_____
Notes:						

Bottling ____/____/____

Spc. Grv. Before Sweeting: _____

Sugar Added: _____

Final pH: _____

Final SO2: _____

Final TA: _____

Of Bottles: _____

% Alcohol By Volume: _____

Attach
Label
Here

Notes: _____

_____

_____

_____

_____

_____

_____

Tasting

Color: _____

Body / Flavor: _____

Finish: _____

Tasting Notes: _____

_____

_____

_____

_____

_____

_____

Other Notes: _____

_____

_____

_____

_____

_____

_____

Primary Fermentation _____/_____/_____   #: _____   Name: _____

Ingredients: _____   Spc. Grv. Before Correcton: _____

_____   Sugar Added: _____

_____   Spc. Grv. After Correction: _____

_____   pH Before Correction: _____

_____   pH Correction: _____

_____   pH After Correction: _____

_____   TA Before: _____

_____   TA Correction: _____

Yeast: _____   TA After: _____

Gallons Of Must: _____   Total SO2: _____

Notes: _____

_____

_____

_____

_____

_____

_____

Secondary Fermentation

Date:	Racked:	Spc. Grv.:	pH:	SO2:	Gallons:	Additions:
____/____/____	☐	_____	_____	_____	_____	_____

Notes: _____

| ____/____/____ | ☐ | _____ | _____ | _____ | _____ | _____ |

Notes: _____

| ____/____/____ | ☐ | _____ | _____ | _____ | _____ | _____ |

Notes: _____

| ____/____/____ | ☐ | _____ | _____ | _____ | _____ | _____ |

Notes: _____

| ____/____/____ | ☐ | _____ | _____ | _____ | _____ | _____ |

Notes: _____

| ____/____/____ | ☐ | _____ | _____ | _____ | _____ | _____ |

Notes: _____

Bottling _____/_____/_____

Spc. Grv. Before Sweeting: _____

Sugar Added: _____

Final pH: _____

Final SO2: _____

Final TA: _____

Of Bottles: _____

% Alcohol By Volume: _____

Attach
Label
Here

Notes: _____

_____

_____

_____

_____

_____

_____

Tasting

Color: _____

Body / Flavor: _____

Finish: _____

Tasting Notes: _____

_____

_____

_____

_____

_____

_____

Other Notes: _____

_____

_____

_____

_____

_____

_____

_____

Primary Fermentation _____/_____/_____   #: _____   Name: _____

Ingredients: _____   Spc. Grv. Before Correcton: _____

_____   Sugar Added: _____

_____   Spc. Grv. After Correction: _____

_____   pH Before Correction: _____

_____   pH Correction: _____

_____   pH After Correction: _____

_____   TA Before: _____

_____   TA Correction: _____

Yeast: _____   TA After: _____

Gallons Of Must: _____   Total SO2: _____

Notes: _____

_____

_____

_____

_____

_____

Secondary Fermentation

Date:	Racked:	Spc. Grv.:	pH:	SO2:	Gallons:	Additions:
____/____/____	☐	_____	_____	_____	_____	_____

Notes: _____

| ____/____/____ | ☐ | _____ | _____ | _____ | _____ | _____ |

Notes: _____

| ____/____/____ | ☐ | _____ | _____ | _____ | _____ | _____ |

Notes: _____

| ____/____/____ | ☐ | _____ | _____ | _____ | _____ | _____ |

Notes: _____

| ____/____/____ | ☐ | _____ | _____ | _____ | _____ | _____ |

Notes: _____

| ____/____/____ | ☐ | _____ | _____ | _____ | _____ | _____ |

Notes: _____

Bottling ____/____/____

Spc. Grv. Before Sweeting: _____

Sugar Added: _____

Final pH: _____

Final SO2: _____

Final TA: _____

Of Bottles: _____

% Alcohol By Volume: _____

Notes: _____

_____

_____

_____

_____

_____

_____

Attach
Label
Here

Tasting

Color: _____

Body / Flavor: _____

Finish: _____

Tasting Notes: _____

_____

_____

_____

_____

_____

_____

Other Notes: _____

_____

_____

_____

_____

_____

_____

_____

Primary Fermentation _____/_____/_____   #: _____   Name: _____

Ingredients: _____   Spc. Grv. Before Correcton: _____

_____   Sugar Added: _____

_____   Spc. Grv. After Correction: _____

_____   pH Before Correction: _____

_____   pH Correction: _____

_____   pH After Correction: _____

_____   TA Before: _____

_____   TA Correction: _____

Yeast: _____   TA After: _____

Gallons Of Must: _____   Total SO2: _____

Notes: _____

_____

_____

_____

_____

_____

Secondary Fermentation

Date:	Racked:	Spc. Grv.:	pH:	SO2:	Gallons:	Additions:
____/____/____	☐	_____	_____	_____	_____	_____
Notes:						
____/____/____	☐	_____	_____	_____	_____	_____
Notes:						
____/____/____	☐	_____	_____	_____	_____	_____
Notes:						
____/____/____	☐	_____	_____	_____	_____	_____
Notes:						
____/____/____	☐	_____	_____	_____	_____	_____
Notes:						
____/____/____	☐	_____	_____	_____	_____	_____
Notes:						

Bottling _____/_____/_____

Spc. Grv. Before Sweeting: _____

Sugar Added: _____

Final pH: _____

Final SO2: _____

Final TA: _____

Of Bottles: _____

% Alcohol By Volume: _____

Notes: _____

_____

_____

_____

_____

_____

_____

Attach
Label
Here

Tasting

Color: _____

Body / Flavor: _____

Finish: _____

Tasting Notes: _____

_____

_____

_____

_____

_____

_____

Other Notes: _____

_____

_____

_____

_____

_____

_____

_____

Primary Fermentation _____/_____/_____   #: _____   Name: _____

Ingredients: _____   Spc. Grv. Before Correcton: _____

_____   Sugar Added: _____

_____   Spc. Grv. After Correction: _____

_____   pH Before Correction: _____

_____   pH Correction: _____

_____   pH After Correction: _____

_____   TA Before: _____

_____   TA Correction: _____

Yeast: _____   TA After: _____

Gallons Of Must: _____   Total SO2: _____

Notes: _____

_____

_____

_____

_____

_____

Secondary Fermentation

Date:	Racked:	Spc. Grv.:	pH:	SO2:	Gallons:	Additions:
_____/_____/_____	☐	_____	_____	_____	_____	_____
Notes:						
_____/_____/_____	☐	_____	_____	_____	_____	_____
Notes:						
_____/_____/_____	☐	_____	_____	_____	_____	_____
Notes:						
_____/_____/_____	☐	_____	_____	_____	_____	_____
Notes:						
_____/_____/_____	☐	_____	_____	_____	_____	_____
Notes:						
_____/_____/_____	☐	_____	_____	_____	_____	_____
Notes:						

Bottling _____/_____/_____

Spc. Grv. Before Sweeting: _____

Sugar Added: _____

Final pH: _____

Final SO2: _____

Final TA: _____

Of Bottles: _____

% Alcohol By Volume: _____

Attach
Label
Here

Notes: _____

_____

_____

_____

_____

_____

_____

Tasting

Color: _____

Body / Flavor: _____

Finish: _____

Tasting Notes: _____

_____

_____

_____

_____

_____

_____

Other Notes: _____

_____

_____

_____

_____

_____

_____

_____

Primary Fermentation _____/_____/_____   #: _____   Name: _____

Ingredients: _____

_____

_____

_____

_____

_____

_____

_____

Yeast: _____

Gallons Of Must: _____

Spc. Grv. Before Correcton: _____

Sugar Added: _____

Spc. Grv. After Correction: _____

pH Before Correction: _____

pH Correction: _____

pH After Correction: _____

TA Before: _____

TA Correction: _____

TA After: _____

Total SO2: _____

Notes: _____

_____

_____

_____

_____

_____

_____

Secondary Fermentation

Date:	Racked:	Spc. Grv.:	pH:	SO2:	Gallons:	Additions:
_____/_____/_____	☐	_____	_____	_____	_____	_____
Notes:						
_____/_____/_____	☐	_____	_____	_____	_____	_____
Notes:						
_____/_____/_____	☐	_____	_____	_____	_____	_____
Notes:						
_____/_____/_____	☐	_____	_____	_____	_____	_____
Notes:						
_____/_____/_____	☐	_____	_____	_____	_____	_____
Notes:						
_____/_____/_____	☐	_____	_____	_____	_____	_____
Notes:						

Bottling _____/_____/_____

Spc. Grv. Before Sweeting: _____

Sugar Added: _____

Final pH: _____

Final SO2: _____

Final TA: _____

Of Bottles: _____

% Alcohol By Volume: _____

Attach
Label
Here

Notes: _____

_____

_____

_____

_____

_____

_____

Tasting

Color: _____

Body / Flavor: _____

Finish: _____

Tasting Notes: _____

_____

_____

_____

_____

_____

_____

Other Notes: _____

_____

_____

_____

_____

_____

_____

_____

Primary Fermentation ____/____/____   #: _____   Name: _____

Ingredients: _____   Spc. Grv. Before Correcton: _____

_____   Sugar Added: _____

_____   Spc. Grv. After Correction: _____

_____   pH Before Correction: _____

_____   pH Correction: _____

_____   pH After Correction: _____

_____   TA Before: _____

_____   TA Correction: _____

Yeast: _____   TA After: _____

Gallons Of Must: _____   Total SO2: _____

Notes: _____

_____

_____

_____

_____

_____

Secondary Fermentation

Date:	Racked:	Spc. Grv.:	pH:	SO2:	Gallons:	Additions:
___/___/___	☐	_____	_____	_____	_____	_____

Notes: _____

| ___/___/___ | ☐ | _____ | _____ | _____ | _____ | _____ |

Notes: _____

| ___/___/___ | ☐ | _____ | _____ | _____ | _____ | _____ |

Notes: _____

| ___/___/___ | ☐ | _____ | _____ | _____ | _____ | _____ |

Notes: _____

| ___/___/___ | ☐ | _____ | _____ | _____ | _____ | _____ |

Notes: _____

| ___/___/___ | ☐ | _____ | _____ | _____ | _____ | _____ |

Notes: _____

Bottling _____/_____/_____

Spc. Grv. Before Sweeting: _____

Sugar Added: _____

Final pH: _____

Final SO2: _____

Final TA: _____

Of Bottles: _____

% Alcohol By Volume: _____

Notes: _____

_____

_____

_____

_____

_____

_____

Attach
Label
Here

Tasting

Color: _____

Body / Flavor: _____

Finish: _____

Tasting Notes: _____

_____

_____

_____

_____

_____

_____

Other Notes: _____

_____

_____

_____

_____

_____

_____

_____

Primary Fermentation ____/____/____   #: _____   Name: _____

Ingredients: _____   Spc. Grv. Before Correcton: _____
_____   Sugar Added: _____
_____   Spc. Grv. After Correction: _____
_____   pH Before Correction: _____
_____   pH Correction: _____
_____   pH After Correction: _____
_____   TA Before: _____
_____   TA Correction: _____
Yeast: _____   TA After: _____
Gallons Of Must: _____   Total SO2: _____
Notes: _____
_____
_____
_____
_____
_____
_____

Secondary Fermentation

Date:	Racked:	Spc. Grv.:	pH:	SO2:	Gallons:	Additions:
___/___/___	☐	_____	_____	_____	_____	_____

Notes: _____

| ___/___/___ | ☐ | _____ | _____ | _____ | _____ | _____ |

Notes: _____

| ___/___/___ | ☐ | _____ | _____ | _____ | _____ | _____ |

Notes: _____

| ___/___/___ | ☐ | _____ | _____ | _____ | _____ | _____ |

Notes: _____

| ___/___/___ | ☐ | _____ | _____ | _____ | _____ | _____ |

Notes: _____

| ___/___/___ | ☐ | _____ | _____ | _____ | _____ | _____ |

Notes: _____

Bottling ____/____/_____

Spc. Grv. Before Sweeting: _____

Sugar Added: _____

Final pH: _____

Final SO2: _____

Final TA: _____

Of Bottles: _____

% Alcohol By Volume: _____

Notes: _____

_____

_____

_____

_____

_____

_____

Attach
Label
Here

Tasting

Color: _____

Body / Flavor: _____

Finish: _____

Tasting Notes: _____

_____

_____

_____

_____

_____

Other Notes: _____

_____

_____

_____

_____

_____

_____

_____

Primary Fermentation ____/____/____   #: _____   Name: _____

Ingredients: _____   Spc. Grv. Before Correcton: _____

_____   Sugar Added: _____

_____   Spc. Grv. After Correction: _____

_____   pH Before Correction: _____

_____   pH Correction: _____

_____   pH After Correction: _____

_____   TA Before: _____

_____   TA Correction: _____

Yeast: _____   TA After: _____

Gallons Of Must: _____   Total SO2: _____

Notes: _____

_____

_____

_____

_____

_____

Secondary Fermentation

Date:	Racked:	Spc. Grv.:	pH:	SO2:	Gallons:	Additions:
____/____/____	☐	_____	_____	_____	_____	_____
Notes:						
____/____/____	☐	_____	_____	_____	_____	_____
Notes:						
____/____/____	☐	_____	_____	_____	_____	_____
Notes:						
____/____/____	☐	_____	_____	_____	_____	_____
Notes:						
____/____/____	☐	_____	_____	_____	_____	_____
Notes:						
____/____/____	☐	_____	_____	_____	_____	_____
Notes:						

Bottling _____/_____/_____

Spc. Grv. Before Sweeting: _____

Sugar Added: _____

Final pH: _____

Final SO2: _____

Final TA: _____

Of Bottles: _____

% Alcohol By Volume: _____

Attach
Label
Here

Notes: _____

_____

_____

_____

_____

_____

_____

Tasting

Color: _____

Body / Flavor: _____

Finish: _____

Tasting Notes: _____

_____

_____

_____

_____

_____

_____

Other Notes: _____

_____

_____

_____

_____

_____

_____

_____

Primary Fermentation _____/_____/_____   #: _____

Ingredients: _____   Name: _____

_____   Spc. Grv. Before Correcton: _____

_____   Sugar Added: _____

_____   Spc. Grv. After Correction: _____

_____   pH Before Correction: _____

_____   pH Correction: _____

_____   pH After Correction: _____

_____   TA Before: _____

_____   TA Correction: _____

Yeast: _____   TA After: _____

Gallons Of Must: _____   Total SO2: _____

Notes: _____

_____

_____

_____

_____

_____

_____

Secondary Fermentation

Date:	Racked:	Spc. Grv.:	pH:	SO2:	Gallons:	Additions:
___/___/___	☐	_____	_____	_____	_____	_____
Notes:						
___/___/___	☐	_____	_____	_____	_____	_____
Notes:						
___/___/___	☐	_____	_____	_____	_____	_____
Notes:						
___/___/___	☐	_____	_____	_____	_____	_____
Notes:						
___/___/___	☐	_____	_____	_____	_____	_____
Notes:						
___/___/___	☐	_____	_____	_____	_____	_____
Notes:						

Bottling _____/_____/_____

Spc. Grv. Before Sweeting: _____

Sugar Added: _____

Final pH: _____

Final SO2: _____

Final TA: _____

Of Bottles: _____

% Alcohol By Volume: _____

Notes: _____

_____

_____

_____

_____

_____

_____

Attach
Label
Here

Tasting

Color: _____

Body / Flavor: _____

Finish: _____

Tasting Notes: _____

_____

_____

_____

_____

_____

_____

Other Notes: _____

_____

_____

_____

_____

_____

_____

_____

Primary Fermentation ____/____/____   #: _____   Name: _____

Ingredients: _____   Spc. Grv. Before Correcton: _____

_____   Sugar Added: _____

_____   Spc. Grv. After Correction: _____

_____   pH Before Correction: _____

_____   pH Correction: _____

_____   pH After Correction: _____

_____   TA Before: _____

_____   TA Correction: _____

Yeast: _____   TA After: _____

Gallons Of Must: _____   Total SO2: _____

Notes: _____

_____

_____

_____

_____

_____

_____

Secondary Fermentation

Date:	Racked:	Spc. Grv.:	pH:	SO2:	Gallons:	Additions:
____/____/____	☐	_____	_____	_____	_____	_____
Notes:						
____/____/____	☐	_____	_____	_____	_____	_____
Notes:						
____/____/____	☐	_____	_____	_____	_____	_____
Notes:						
____/____/____	☐	_____	_____	_____	_____	_____
Notes:						
____/____/____	☐	_____	_____	_____	_____	_____
Notes:						
____/____/____	☐	_____	_____	_____	_____	_____
Notes:						

Bottling _____/_____/_____

Spc. Grv. Before Sweeting: _____

Sugar Added: _____

Final pH: _____

Final SO2: _____

Final TA: _____

Of Bottles: _____

% Alcohol By Volume: _____

Attach
Label
Here

Notes: _____

_____

_____

_____

_____

_____

_____

Tasting

Color: _____

Body / Flavor: _____

Finish: _____

Tasting Notes: _____

_____

_____

_____

_____

_____

Other Notes: _____

_____

_____

_____

_____

_____

_____

Primary Fermentation _____/_____/_____   #: _____   Name: _____

Ingredients: _____   Spc. Grv. Before Correcton: _____

_____   Sugar Added: _____

_____   Spc. Grv. After Correction: _____

_____   pH Before Correction: _____

_____   pH Correction: _____

_____   pH After Correction: _____

_____   TA Before: _____

_____   TA Correction: _____

Yeast: _____   TA After: _____

Gallons Of Must: _____   Total SO2: _____

Notes: _____

_____

_____

_____

_____

_____

Secondary Fermentation

Date:	Racked:	Spc. Grv.:	pH:	SO2:	Gallons:	Additions:
___/___/___	☐	_____	_____	_____	_____	_____

Notes: _____

| ___/___/___ | ☐ | _____ | _____ | _____ | _____ | _____ |

Notes: _____

| ___/___/___ | ☐ | _____ | _____ | _____ | _____ | _____ |

Notes: _____

| ___/___/___ | ☐ | _____ | _____ | _____ | _____ | _____ |

Notes: _____

| ___/___/___ | ☐ | _____ | _____ | _____ | _____ | _____ |

Notes: _____

| ___/___/___ | ☐ | _____ | _____ | _____ | _____ | _____ |

Notes: _____

Bottling _____/_____/_____

Spc. Grv. Before Sweeting: _____

Sugar Added: _____

Final pH: _____

Final SO2: _____

Final TA: _____

Of Bottles: _____

% Alcohol By Volume: _____

Notes: _____

_____

_____

_____

_____

Attach
Label
Here

_____

_____

Tasting

Color: _____

Body / Flavor: _____

Finish: _____

Tasting Notes: _____

_____

_____

_____

_____

_____

_____

Other Notes: _____

_____

_____

_____

_____

_____

_____

_____

Primary Fermentation _____/_____/_____   #: _____

Ingredients: _____

_____

_____

_____

_____

_____

_____

Yeast: _____

Gallons Of Must: _____

Notes: _____

_____

_____

_____

_____

_____

Name: _____

Spc. Grv. Before Correcton: _____

Sugar Added: _____

Spc. Grv. After Correction: _____

pH Before Correction: _____

pH Correction: _____

pH After Correction: _____

TA Before: _____

TA Correction: _____

TA After: _____

Total SO2: _____

Secondary Fermentation

Date:	Racked:	Spc. Grv.:	pH:	SO2:	Gallons:	Additions:
_____/_____/_____	☐	_____	_____	_____	_____	_____
Notes:						
_____/_____/_____	☐	_____	_____	_____	_____	_____
Notes:						
_____/_____/_____	☐	_____	_____	_____	_____	_____
Notes:						
_____/_____/_____	☐	_____	_____	_____	_____	_____
Notes:						
_____/_____/_____	☐	_____	_____	_____	_____	_____
Notes:						
_____/_____/_____	☐	_____	_____	_____	_____	_____
Notes:						

Bottling _____/_____/_____

Spc. Grv. Before Sweeting: _____

Sugar Added: _____

Final pH: _____

Final SO2: _____

Final TA: _____

Of Bottles: _____

% Alcohol By Volume: _____

Notes: _____

_____

_____

_____

_____

_____

_____

Attach
Label
Here

Tasting

Color: _____

Body / Flavor: _____

Finish: _____

Tasting Notes: _____

_____

_____

_____

_____

_____

Other Notes: _____

_____

_____

_____

_____

_____

_____

Primary Fermentation _____/_____/_____   #: _____   Name: _____

Ingredients: _____   Spc. Grv. Before Correcton: _____

_____   Sugar Added: _____

_____   Spc. Grv. After Correction: _____

_____   pH Before Correction: _____

_____   pH Correction: _____

_____   pH After Correction: _____

_____   TA Before: _____

_____   TA Correction: _____

Yeast: _____   TA After: _____

Gallons Of Must: _____   Total SO2: _____

Notes: _____

_____

_____

_____

_____

_____

_____

Secondary Fermentation

Date:	Racked:	Spc. Grv.:	pH:	SO2:	Gallons:	Additions:
____/____/____	☐	_____	_____	_____	_____	_____
Notes:						
____/____/____	☐	_____	_____	_____	_____	_____
Notes:						
____/____/____	☐	_____	_____	_____	_____	_____
Notes:						
____/____/____	☐	_____	_____	_____	_____	_____
Notes:						
____/____/____	☐	_____	_____	_____	_____	_____
Notes:						
____/____/____	☐	_____	_____	_____	_____	_____
Notes:						

Bottling _____/_____/_____

Spc. Grv. Before Sweeting: _____

Sugar Added: _____

Final pH: _____

Final SO2: _____

Final TA: _____

Of Bottles: _____

% Alcohol By Volume: _____

Notes: _____

_____

_____

_____

_____

_____

_____

Attach
Label
Here

Tasting

Color: _____

Body / Flavor: _____

Finish: _____

Tasting Notes: _____

_____

_____

_____

_____

_____

_____

Other Notes: _____

_____

_____

_____

_____

_____

_____

_____

Primary Fermentation _____/_____/_____   #: _____   Name: _____

Ingredients: _____   Spc. Grv. Before Correcton: _____

_____   Sugar Added: _____

_____   Spc. Grv. After Correction: _____

_____   pH Before Correction: _____

_____   pH Correction: _____

_____   pH After Correction: _____

_____   TA Before: _____

_____   TA Correction: _____

Yeast: _____   TA After: _____

Gallons Of Must: _____   Total SO2: _____

Notes: _____

_____

_____

_____

_____

_____

Secondary Fermentation

Date:	Racked:	Spc. Grv.:	pH:	SO2:	Gallons:	Additions:
____/____/____	☐	_____	_____	_____	_____	_____
Notes:						
____/____/____	☐	_____	_____	_____	_____	_____
Notes:						
____/____/____	☐	_____	_____	_____	_____	_____
Notes:						
____/____/____	☐	_____	_____	_____	_____	_____
Notes:						
____/____/____	☐	_____	_____	_____	_____	_____
Notes:						
____/____/____	☐	_____	_____	_____	_____	_____
Notes:						

Bottling _____/_____/_____

Spc. Grv. Before Sweeting: _____

Sugar Added: _____

Final pH: _____

Final SO2: _____

Final TA: _____

Of Bottles: _____

% Alcohol By Volume: _____

Notes: _____

_____

_____

_____

_____

_____

_____

Attach
Label
Here

Tasting

Color: _____

Body / Flavor: _____

Finish: _____

Tasting Notes: _____

_____

_____

_____

_____

_____

_____

Other Notes: _____

_____

_____

_____

_____

_____

_____

_____

_____

Primary Fermentation _____/_____/_____   #: _____

Ingredients: _____

_____

_____

_____

_____

_____

_____

Yeast: _____

Gallons Of Must: _____

Notes: _____

_____

_____

_____

_____

_____

_____

Name: _____

Spc. Grv. Before Correcton: _____

Sugar Added: _____

Spc. Grv. After Correction: _____

pH Before Correction: _____

pH Correction: _____

pH After Correction: _____

TA Before: _____

TA Correction: _____

TA After: _____

Total SO2: _____

Secondary Fermentation

Date:	Racked:	Spc. Grv.:	pH:	SO2:	Gallons:	Additions:
_____/_____/_____	☐	_____	_____	_____	_____	_____
Notes:						
_____/_____/_____	☐	_____	_____	_____	_____	_____
Notes:						
_____/_____/_____	☐	_____	_____	_____	_____	_____
Notes:						
_____/_____/_____	☐	_____	_____	_____	_____	_____
Notes:						
_____/_____/_____	☐	_____	_____	_____	_____	_____
Notes:						
_____/_____/_____	☐	_____	_____	_____	_____	_____
Notes:						

Bottling _____/_____/_____

Spc. Grv. Before Sweeting: _____

Sugar Added: _____

Final pH: _____

Final SO2: _____

Final TA: _____

Of Bottles: _____

% Alcohol By Volume: _____

Notes: _____

_____

_____

_____

_____

_____

_____

Attach
Label
Here

Tasting

Color: _____

Body / Flavor: _____

Finish: _____

Tasting Notes: _____

_____

_____

_____

_____

_____

_____

Other Notes: _____

_____

_____

_____

_____

_____

_____

_____

Primary Fermentation _____/_____/_____   #: _____

Ingredients: _____

_____

_____

_____

_____

_____

_____

_____

Yeast: _____

Gallons Of Must: _____

Notes: _____

_____

_____

_____

_____

_____

_____

Name: _____

Spc. Grv. Before Correcton: _____

Sugar Added: _____

Spc. Grv. After Correction: _____

pH Before Correction: _____

pH Correction: _____

pH After Correction: _____

TA Before: _____

TA Correction: _____

TA After: _____

Total SO2: _____

Secondary Fermentation

Date:	Racked:	Spc. Grv.:	pH:	SO2:	Gallons:	Additions:
____/____/____	☐	_____	_____	_____	_____	_____
Notes:						
____/____/____	☐	_____	_____	_____	_____	_____
Notes:						
____/____/____	☐	_____	_____	_____	_____	_____
Notes:						
____/____/____	☐	_____	_____	_____	_____	_____
Notes:						
____/____/____	☐	_____	_____	_____	_____	_____
Notes:						
____/____/____	☐	_____	_____	_____	_____	_____
Notes:						

Bottling ____/____/____

Spc. Grv. Before Sweeting: _____

Sugar Added: _____

Final pH: _____

Final SO2: _____

Final TA: _____

Of Bottles: _____

% Alcohol By Volume: _____

Attach
Label
Here

Notes: _____

_____

_____

_____

_____

_____

_____

Tasting

Color: _____

Body / Flavor: _____

Finish: _____

Tasting Notes: _____

_____

_____

_____

_____

_____

_____

Other Notes: _____

_____

_____

_____

_____

_____

_____

_____

_____

Primary Fermentation _____/_____/_____   #: _____   Name: _____

Ingredients: _____   Spc. Grv. Before Correcton: _____

_____   Sugar Added: _____

_____   Spc. Grv. After Correction: _____

_____   pH Before Correction: _____

_____   pH Correction: _____

_____   pH After Correction: _____

_____   TA Before: _____

_____   TA Correction: _____

Yeast: _____   TA After: _____

Gallons Of Must: _____   Total SO2: _____

Notes: _____

_____

_____

_____

_____

_____

Secondary Fermentation

Date:	Racked:	Spc. Grv.:	pH:	SO2:	Gallons:	Additions:
___/___/___	☐	_____	_____	_____	_____	_____

Notes: _____

| ___/___/___ | ☐ | _____ | _____ | _____ | _____ | _____ |

Notes: _____

| ___/___/___ | ☐ | _____ | _____ | _____ | _____ | _____ |

Notes: _____

| ___/___/___ | ☐ | _____ | _____ | _____ | _____ | _____ |

Notes: _____

| ___/___/___ | ☐ | _____ | _____ | _____ | _____ | _____ |

Notes: _____

| ___/___/___ | ☐ | _____ | _____ | _____ | _____ | _____ |

Notes: _____

Bottling _____/_____/_____

Spc. Grv. Before Sweeting: _____

Sugar Added: _____

Final pH: _____

Final SO2: _____

Final TA: _____

Of Bottles: _____

% Alcohol By Volume: _____

Notes: _____

_____

_____

_____

_____

_____

_____

Attach
Label
Here

Tasting

Color: _____

Body / Flavor: _____

Finish: _____

Tasting Notes: _____

_____

_____

_____

_____

_____

_____

Other Notes: _____

_____

_____

_____

_____

_____

_____

_____

Primary Fermentation _____/_____/_____   #: _____   Name: _____

Ingredients: _____   Spc. Grv. Before Correcton: _____

_____   Sugar Added: _____

_____   Spc. Grv. After Correction: _____

_____   pH Before Correction: _____

_____   pH Correction: _____

_____   pH After Correction: _____

_____   TA Before: _____

_____   TA Correction: _____

Yeast: _____   TA After: _____

Gallons Of Must: _____   Total SO2: _____

Notes: _____

_____

_____

_____

_____

_____

Secondary Fermentation

Date:	Racked:	Spc. Grv.:	pH:	SO2:	Gallons:	Additions:
____/____/____	☐	_____	_____	_____	_____	_____
Notes:						
____/____/____	☐	_____	_____	_____	_____	_____
Notes:						
____/____/____	☐	_____	_____	_____	_____	_____
Notes:						
____/____/____	☐	_____	_____	_____	_____	_____
Notes:						
____/____/____	☐	_____	_____	_____	_____	_____
Notes:						
____/____/____	☐	_____	_____	_____	_____	_____
Notes:						

Bottling _____/_____/_____

Spc. Grv. Before Sweeting: _____

Sugar Added: _____

Final pH: _____

Final SO2: _____

Final TA: _____

Of Bottles: _____

% Alcohol By Volume: _____

Notes: _____

_____

_____

_____

_____

_____

_____

Attach
Label
Here

Tasting

Color: _____

Body / Flavor: _____

Finish: _____

Tasting Notes: _____

_____

_____

_____

_____

_____

Other Notes: _____

_____

_____

_____

_____

_____

_____

_____

Primary Fermentation ____/____/____   #: _____   Name: _____

Ingredients: _____

_____

_____

_____

_____

_____

_____

Yeast: _____

Gallons Of Must: _____

Notes: _____

_____

_____

_____

_____

_____

_____

Spc. Grv. Before Correcton: _____

Sugar Added: _____

Spc. Grv. After Correction: _____

pH Before Correction: _____

pH Correction: _____

pH After Correction: _____

TA Before: _____

TA Correction: _____

TA After: _____

Total SO2: _____

Secondary Fermentation

Date:	Racked:	Spc. Grv.:	pH:	SO2:	Gallons:	Additions:
____/____/____	☐	_____	_____	_____	_____	_____
Notes:						
____/____/____	☐	_____	_____	_____	_____	_____
Notes:						
____/____/____	☐	_____	_____	_____	_____	_____
Notes:						
____/____/____	☐	_____	_____	_____	_____	_____
Notes:						
____/____/____	☐	_____	_____	_____	_____	_____
Notes:						
____/____/____	☐	_____	_____	_____	_____	_____
Notes:						

Bottling ____/____/____

Spc. Grv. Before Sweeting: _____

Sugar Added: _____

Final pH: _____

Final SO2: _____

Final TA: _____

Of Bottles: _____

% Alcohol By Volume: _____

Notes: _____

_____

_____

_____

_____

_____

_____

Attach
Label
Here

Tasting

Color: _____

Body / Flavor: _____

Finish: _____

Tasting Notes: _____

_____

_____

_____

_____

_____

_____

Other Notes: _____

_____

_____

_____

_____

_____

_____

_____

Primary Fermentation ____/____/____   #: _____   Name: _____

Ingredients: _____   Spc. Grv. Before Correcton: _____

_____   Sugar Added: _____

_____   Spc. Grv. After Correction: _____

_____   pH Before Correction: _____

_____   pH Correction: _____

_____   pH After Correction: _____

_____   TA Before: _____

_____   TA Correction: _____

Yeast: _____   TA After: _____

Gallons Of Must: _____   Total SO2: _____

Notes: _____

_____

_____

_____

_____

_____

Secondary Fermentation

Date:	Racked:	Spc. Grv.:	pH:	SO2:	Gallons:	Additions:
____/____/____	☐	_____	_____	_____	_____	_____

Notes: _____

| ____/____/____ | ☐ | _____ | _____ | _____ | _____ | _____ |

Notes: _____

| ____/____/____ | ☐ | _____ | _____ | _____ | _____ | _____ |

Notes: _____

| ____/____/____ | ☐ | _____ | _____ | _____ | _____ | _____ |

Notes: _____

| ____/____/____ | ☐ | _____ | _____ | _____ | _____ | _____ |

Notes: _____

| ____/____/____ | ☐ | _____ | _____ | _____ | _____ | _____ |

Notes: _____

Bottling _____/_____/_____

Spc. Grv. Before Sweeting: _____

Sugar Added: _____

Final pH: _____

Final SO2: _____

Final TA: _____

Of Bottles: _____

% Alcohol By Volume: _____

Notes: _____

_____

_____

_____

_____

_____

_____

Attach
Label
Here

Tasting

Color: _____

Body / Flavor: _____

Finish: _____

Tasting Notes: _____

_____

_____

_____

_____

_____

_____

Other Notes: _____

_____

_____

_____

_____

_____

_____

_____

Primary Fermentation _____/_____/_____   #: _____   Name: _____

Ingredients: _____   Spc. Grv. Before Correcton: _____

_____   Sugar Added: _____

_____   Spc. Grv. After Correction: _____

_____   pH Before Correction: _____

_____   pH Correction: _____

_____   pH After Correction: _____

_____   TA Before: _____

_____   TA Correction: _____

Yeast: _____   TA After: _____

Gallons Of Must: _____   Total SO2: _____

Notes: _____

_____

_____

_____

_____

_____

Secondary Fermentation

Date:	Racked:	Spc. Grv.:	pH:	SO2:	Gallons:	Additions:
___/___/___	☐	_____	_____	_____	_____	_____

Notes: _____

| ___/___/___ | ☐ | _____ | _____ | _____ | _____ | _____ |

Notes: _____

| ___/___/___ | ☐ | _____ | _____ | _____ | _____ | _____ |

Notes: _____

| ___/___/___ | ☐ | _____ | _____ | _____ | _____ | _____ |

Notes: _____

| ___/___/___ | ☐ | _____ | _____ | _____ | _____ | _____ |

Notes: _____

| ___/___/___ | ☐ | _____ | _____ | _____ | _____ | _____ |

Notes: _____

Bottling ____/____/____

Spc. Grv. Before Sweeting: _____

Sugar Added: _____

Final pH: _____

Final SO2: _____

Final TA: _____

Of Bottles: _____

% Alcohol By Volume: _____

Attach
Label
Here

Notes: _____

_____

_____

_____

_____

_____

_____

Tasting

Color: _____

Body / Flavor: _____

Finish: _____

Tasting Notes: _____

_____

_____

_____

_____

_____

_____

Other Notes: _____

_____

_____

_____

_____

_____

_____

_____

Primary Fermentation _____/_____/_____   #: _____   Name: _____

Ingredients: _____   Spc. Grv. Before Correcton: _____

_____   Sugar Added: _____

_____   Spc. Grv. After Correction: _____

_____   pH Before Correction: _____

_____   pH Correction: _____

_____   pH After Correction: _____

_____   TA Before: _____

_____   TA Correction: _____

Yeast: _____   TA After: _____

Gallons Of Must: _____   Total SO2: _____

Notes: _____

_____

_____

_____

_____

_____

_____

Secondary Fermentation

Date:	Racked:	Spc. Grv.:	pH:	SO2:	Gallons:	Additions:
___/___/___	☐	_____	_____	_____	_____	_____
Notes:						
___/___/___	☐	_____	_____	_____	_____	_____
Notes:						
___/___/___	☐	_____	_____	_____	_____	_____
Notes:						
___/___/___	☐	_____	_____	_____	_____	_____
Notes:						
___/___/___	☐	_____	_____	_____	_____	_____
Notes:						
___/___/___	☐	_____	_____	_____	_____	_____
Notes:						

Bottling __ __ / ____ / ____

Spc. Grv. Before Sweeting: _____

Sugar Added: _____

Final pH: _____

Final SO2: _____

Final TA: _____

Of Bottles: _____

% Alcohol By Volume: _____

Notes: _____

_____

_____

_____

_____

_____

_____

Attach
Label
Here

Tasting

Color: _____

Body / Flavor: _____

Finish: _____

Tasting Notes: _____

_____

_____

_____

_____

_____

_____

Other Notes: _____

_____

_____

_____

_____

_____

_____

_____

To Stabalize Wine: (Per Gallon)

1/2 tsp Potassium Sorbate

1 Crushed Campden Tablet

Yeast Starter Recipe:

Ingredients: (For a 5 gallon batch of wine)

3 ounces frozen 100% orange juice concentrate (no preservatives)

24 ounces water

3/4 cup of sugar

2 rounded teaspoons of ordinary yeast nutrient

1 packet of yeast. (Lalvin K1-V1116 or EC-1118 works very well)

Heat the water, frozen orange juice, and sugar in a 2-quart saucepan. When the mix boils, remove it from the heat, add the nutrient, and cover the saucepan. Cool the mix to room temperature (an ice bath may be used).

Transfer the starter mix to a sterilized 1-gallon jug (or an erlynmeyer flask). Add the yeast culture and attach an air lock. After 2 to 6 hours when the solution is in an active ferment (much CO_2 is expelled through the air lock when swirled) it is ready to add to the must.

Special Thanks to:

The House Of Homebrew at http://www.houseofhomebrew.com/

7/21/08 Japanese Beetles finished-gone

7/22/08 Went thru Feder vineyard-found black
rot + some bunch rot- cleaned up
bunches + exposed bunches to sunlight
+ air flow.

9/2/08 Feder vines decimated by birds-no
grapes left.
Tasted a few left + go readings +
Brix 22°-24° WOW.
in 2009:
1) protect against rot; however bunches
do not appear lightly packed as are
Aurel.
2) Consider Netting + insect Traps
at end of July before going to ADK
3) Prepare to make wine last week
of August to Sept 1 or 2.
9/2/09 Brix 11½°
9/7/09 Brix
Seyval Brix from 13¾ to 14½°

Summer 09 July Lots rain then dry August
Hard to spray early as rainy
Frammette lots growth few grapes
Feder no grapes but abundant growth,
my pruning needs massive study.
Sept- dry good sun.
Japanese Beetles nonexistent almost

9/14/09 Brix from a broad sample 15¼°

9/22/09 juice at 15-14½° Seyval-
Just no sustained heat

9/30/09 Seyval Brix at 16°. Must pick
on 0/5

Your Notes

Your Notes

Your Notes

Your Notes

Your Notes

Your Notes

Your Notes

Your Notes

Your Notes

Your Notes

Carboy Tag

Name: _____ #: _____

Start Date: _____ / _____ / _____

Next Racking Date: Spc. Grv. / Note:

_____ / _____ / _____

_____ / _____ / _____

_____ / _____ / _____

_____ / _____ / _____

_____ / _____ / _____

_____ / _____ / _____

Carboy Tag

Name: _____ #: _____

Start Date: _____ / _____ / _____

Next Racking Date: Spc. Grv. / Note:

_____ / _____ / _____

_____ / _____ / _____

_____ / _____ / _____

_____ / _____ / _____

_____ / _____ / _____

_____ / _____ / _____

Carboy Tag

Name: _____ #: _____

Start Date: _____ / _____ / _____

Next Racking Date: Spc. Grv. / Note:

_____ / _____ / _____

_____ / _____ / _____

_____ / _____ / _____

_____ / _____ / _____

_____ / _____ / _____

_____ / _____ / _____

Carboy Tag

Name: _____ #: _____

Start Date: _____ / _____ / _____

Next Racking Date: Spc. Grv. / Note:

_____ / _____ / _____

_____ / _____ / _____

_____ / _____ / _____

_____ / _____ / _____

_____ / _____ / _____

_____ / _____ / _____

Carboy Tag

Name: _____ #: _____

Start Date: _____ / _____ / _____

Next Racking Date: Spc. Grv. / Note:

_____ / _____ / _____

_____ / _____ / _____

_____ / _____ / _____

_____ / _____ / _____

_____ / _____ / _____

_____ / _____ / _____

Carboy Tag

Name: _____ #: _____

Start Date: _____ / _____ / _____

Next Racking Date: Spc. Grv. / Note:

_____ / _____ / _____

_____ / _____ / _____

_____ / _____ / _____

_____ / _____ / _____

_____ / _____ / _____

_____ / _____ / _____

Carboy Tag

Name: _____ #: _____

Start Date: _____ / _____ / _____

Next Racking Date: Spc. Grv. / Note:

_____ / _____ / _____

_____ / _____ / _____

_____ / _____ / _____

_____ / _____ / _____

_____ / _____ / _____

_____ / _____ / _____

Carboy Tag

Name: _____ #: _____

Start Date: _____ / _____ / _____

Next Racking Date: Spc. Grv. / Note:

_____ / _____ / _____

_____ / _____ / _____

_____ / _____ / _____

_____ / _____ / _____

_____ / _____ / _____

_____ / _____ / _____

Carboy Tag

Name: _____ #: _____

Start Date: _____ / _____ / _____

Next Racking Date: Spc. Grv. / Note:

_____ / _____ / _____

_____ / _____ / _____

_____ / _____ / _____

_____ / _____ / _____

_____ / _____ / _____

_____ / _____ / _____

Carboy Tag

Name: _____ #: _____

Start Date: _____ / _____ / _____

Next Racking Date: Spc. Grv. / Note:

_____ / _____ / _____

_____ / _____ / _____

_____ / _____ / _____

_____ / _____ / _____

_____ / _____ / _____

_____ / _____ / _____

Carboy Tag

Name: _____ #: _____

Start Date: _____ / _____ / _____

Next Racking Date: Spc. Grv. / Note:

_____ / _____ / _____

_____ / _____ / _____

_____ / _____ / _____

_____ / _____ / _____

_____ / _____ / _____

_____ / _____ / _____

Carboy Tag

Name: _____ #: _____

Start Date: _____ / _____ / _____

Next Racking Date: Spc. Grv. / Note:

_____ / _____ / _____

_____ / _____ / _____

_____ / _____ / _____

_____ / _____ / _____

_____ / _____ / _____

_____ / _____ / _____

Carboy Tag

Name: _____ #: _____

Start Date: _____ / _____ / _____

Next Racking Date: Spc. Grv. / Note:

_____ / _____ _____

_____ / _____ _____

_____ / _____ _____

_____ / _____ _____

_____ / _____ _____

_____ / _____ _____

Carboy Tag

Name: _____ #: _____

Start Date: _____ / _____ / _____

Next Racking Date: Spc. Grv. / Note:

_____ / _____ _____

_____ / _____ _____

_____ / _____ _____

_____ / _____ _____

_____ / _____ _____

_____ / _____ _____

Carboy Tag

Name: _____ #: _____

Start Date: _____ / _____ / _____

Next Racking Date: Spc. Grv. / Note:

_____ / _____ _____

_____ / _____ _____

_____ / _____ _____

_____ / _____ _____

_____ / _____ _____

_____ / _____ _____

Carboy Tag

Name: _____ #: _____

Start Date: _____ / _____ / _____

Next Racking Date: Spc. Grv. / Note:

_____ / _____ _____

_____ / _____ _____

_____ / _____ _____

_____ / _____ _____

_____ / _____ _____

_____ / _____ _____

Carboy Tag

Name: _____ #: _____

Start Date: _____ / _____ / _____

Next Racking Date: Spc. Grv. / Note:

_____ / _____ _____

_____ / _____ _____

_____ / _____ _____

_____ / _____ _____

_____ / _____ _____

_____ / _____ _____

Carboy Tag

Name: _____ #: _____

Start Date: _____ / _____ / _____

Next Racking Date: Spc. Grv. / Note:

_____ / _____ _____

_____ / _____ _____

_____ / _____ _____

_____ / _____ _____

_____ / _____ _____

_____ / _____ _____

Carboy Tag

Name: _____ #: _____

Start Date: _____ / _____ / _____

Next Racking Date: Spc. Grv. / Note:

_____ / _____ / _____

_____ / _____ / _____

_____ / _____ / _____

_____ / _____ / _____

_____ / _____ / _____

_____ / _____ / _____

Carboy Tag

Name: _____ #: _____

Start Date: _____ / _____ / _____

Next Racking Date: Spc. Grv. / Note:

_____ / _____ / _____

_____ / _____ / _____

_____ / _____ / _____

_____ / _____ / _____

_____ / _____ / _____

_____ / _____ / _____

Carboy Tag

Name: _____ #: _____

Start Date: _____ / _____ / _____

Next Racking Date: Spc. Grv. / Note:

_____ / _____ / _____

_____ / _____ / _____

_____ / _____ / _____

_____ / _____ / _____

_____ / _____ / _____

_____ / _____ / _____

Carboy Tag

Name: _____ #: _____

Start Date: _____ / _____ / _____

Next Racking Date: Spc. Grv. / Note:

_____ / _____ / _____

_____ / _____ / _____

_____ / _____ / _____

_____ / _____ / _____

_____ / _____ / _____

_____ / _____ / _____

Carboy Tag

Name: _____ #: _____

Start Date: _____ / _____ / _____

Next Racking Date: Spc. Grv. / Note:

_____ / _____ / _____

_____ / _____ / _____

_____ / _____ / _____

_____ / _____ / _____

_____ / _____ / _____

_____ / _____ / _____

Carboy Tag

Name: _____ #: _____

Start Date: _____ / _____ / _____

Next Racking Date: Spc. Grv. / Note:

_____ / _____ / _____

_____ / _____ / _____

_____ / _____ / _____

_____ / _____ / _____

_____ / _____ / _____

_____ / _____ / _____

Carboy Tag

Name: #:

Start Date: /   /

Next Racking Date: Spc. Grv. / Note:

        /   /

        /   /

        /   /

        /   /

        /   /

        /   /

Carboy Tag

Name: #:

Start Date: /   /

Next Racking Date: Spc. Grv. / Note:

        /   /

        /   /

        /   /

        /   /

        /   /

        /   /

Carboy Tag

Name: #:

Start Date: /   /

Next Racking Date: Spc. Grv. / Note:

        /   /

        /   /

        /   /

        /   /

        /   /

        /   /

Carboy Tag

Name: #:

Start Date: /   /

Next Racking Date: Spc. Grv. / Note:

        /   /

        /   /

        /   /

        /   /

        /   /

        /   /

Carboy Tag

Name: #:

Start Date: /   /

Next Racking Date: Spc. Grv. / Note:

        /   /

        /   /

        /   /

        /   /

        /   /

        /   /

Carboy Tag

Name: #:

Start Date: /   /

Next Racking Date: Spc. Grv. / Note:

        /   /

        /   /

        /   /

        /   /

        /   /

        /   /

Carboy Tag

Name: _____ #: _____

Start Date: _____ / _____ / _____

Next Racking Date: Spc. Grv. / Note:

_____ / _____ / _____

_____ / _____ / _____

_____ / _____ / _____

_____ / _____ / _____

_____ / _____ / _____

_____ / _____ / _____

Carboy Tag

Name: _____ #: _____

Start Date: _____ / _____ / _____

Next Racking Date: Spc. Grv. / Note:

_____ / _____ / _____

_____ / _____ / _____

_____ / _____ / _____

_____ / _____ / _____

_____ / _____ / _____

_____ / _____ / _____

Carboy Tag

Name: _____ #: _____

Start Date: _____ / _____ / _____

Next Racking Date: Spc. Grv. / Note:

_____ / _____ / _____

_____ / _____ / _____

_____ / _____ / _____

_____ / _____ / _____

_____ / _____ / _____

_____ / _____ / _____

Carboy Tag

Name: _____ #: _____

Start Date: _____ / _____ / _____

Next Racking Date: Spc. Grv. / Note:

_____ / _____ / _____

_____ / _____ / _____

_____ / _____ / _____

_____ / _____ / _____

_____ / _____ / _____

_____ / _____ / _____

Carboy Tag

Name: _____ #: _____

Start Date: _____ / _____ / _____

Next Racking Date: Spc. Grv. / Note:

_____ / _____ / _____

_____ / _____ / _____

_____ / _____ / _____

_____ / _____ / _____

_____ / _____ / _____

_____ / _____ / _____

Carboy Tag

Name: _____ #: _____

Start Date: _____ / _____ / _____

Next Racking Date: Spc. Grv. / Note:

_____ / _____ / _____

_____ / _____ / _____

_____ / _____ / _____

_____ / _____ / _____

_____ / _____ / _____

_____ / _____ / _____

Carboy Tag

Name: _____ #: _____

Start Date: _____ / _____ / _____

Next Racking Date: Spc. Grv. / Note:

_____ / _____ / _____

_____ / _____ / _____

_____ / _____ / _____

_____ / _____ / _____

_____ / _____ / _____

_____ / _____ / _____

Carboy Tag

Name: _____ #: _____

Start Date: _____ / _____ / _____

Next Racking Date: Spc. Grv. / Note:

_____ / _____ / _____

_____ / _____ / _____

_____ / _____ / _____

_____ / _____ / _____

_____ / _____ / _____

_____ / _____ / _____

Carboy Tag

Name: _____ #: _____

Start Date: _____ / _____ / _____

Next Racking Date: Spc. Grv. / Note:

_____ / _____ / _____

_____ / _____ / _____

_____ / _____ / _____

_____ / _____ / _____

_____ / _____ / _____

_____ / _____ / _____

Carboy Tag

Name: _____ #: _____

Start Date: _____ / _____ / _____

Next Racking Date: Spc. Grv. / Note:

_____ / _____ / _____

_____ / _____ / _____

_____ / _____ / _____

_____ / _____ / _____

_____ / _____ / _____

_____ / _____ / _____

Carboy Tag

Name: _____ #: _____

Start Date: _____ / _____ / _____

Next Racking Date: Spc. Grv. / Note:

_____ / _____ / _____

_____ / _____ / _____

_____ / _____ / _____

_____ / _____ / _____

_____ / _____ / _____

_____ / _____ / _____

Carboy Tag

Name: _____ #: _____

Start Date: _____ / _____ / _____

Next Racking Date: Spc. Grv. / Note:

_____ / _____ / _____

_____ / _____ / _____

_____ / _____ / _____

_____ / _____ / _____

_____ / _____ / _____

_____ / _____ / _____

Carboy Tag

Name: _____ #: _____

Start Date: _____ / _____ / _____

Next Racking Date: Spc. Grv. / Note:

_____ / _____ / _____

_____ / _____ / _____

_____ / _____ / _____

_____ / _____ / _____

_____ / _____ / _____

_____ / _____ / _____

Carboy Tag

Name: _____ #: _____

Start Date: _____ / _____ / _____

Next Racking Date: Spc. Grv. / Note:

_____ / _____ / _____

_____ / _____ / _____

_____ / _____ / _____

_____ / _____ / _____

_____ / _____ / _____

_____ / _____ / _____

Carboy Tag

Name: _____ #: _____

Start Date: _____ / _____ / _____

Next Racking Date: Spc. Grv. / Note:

_____ / _____ / _____

_____ / _____ / _____

_____ / _____ / _____

_____ / _____ / _____

_____ / _____ / _____

_____ / _____ / _____

Carboy Tag

Name: _____ #: _____

Start Date: _____ / _____ / _____

Next Racking Date: Spc. Grv. / Note:

_____ / _____ / _____

_____ / _____ / _____

_____ / _____ / _____

_____ / _____ / _____

_____ / _____ / _____

_____ / _____ / _____

Carboy Tag

Name: _____ #: _____

Start Date: _____ / _____ / _____

Next Racking Date: Spc. Grv. / Note:

_____ / _____ / _____

_____ / _____ / _____

_____ / _____ / _____

_____ / _____ / _____

_____ / _____ / _____

_____ / _____ / _____

Carboy Tag

Name: _____ #: _____

Start Date: _____ / _____ / _____

Next Racking Date: Spc. Grv. / Note:

_____ / _____ / _____

_____ / _____ / _____

_____ / _____ / _____

_____ / _____ / _____

_____ / _____ / _____

_____ / _____ / _____

Carboy Tag

Name: _____ #: _____

Start Date: _____ / _____ / _____

Next Racking Date: Spc. Grv. / Note:

_____ / _____ / _____

_____ / _____ / _____

_____ / _____ / _____

_____ / _____ / _____

_____ / _____ / _____

_____ / _____ / _____

Carboy Tag

Name: _____ #: _____

Start Date: _____ / _____ / _____

Next Racking Date: Spc. Grv. / Note:

_____ / _____ / _____

_____ / _____ / _____

_____ / _____ / _____

_____ / _____ / _____

_____ / _____ / _____

_____ / _____ / _____

Printed in the United States
112885LV00006B/41-42/A